THE ART OF INVESTIGATIVE INTERVIEWING

THE ART OF INVESTIGATIVE INTERVIEWING

A Human Approach to Testimonial Evidence

Second Edition

Charles L. Yeschke

BUTTERWORTH HEINEMANN

An imprint of Elsevier Science

Amsterdam   Boston   London   New York   Oxford   Paris
San Diego   San Francisco   Singapore   Sydney   Tokyo

Butterworth–Heinemann is an imprint of Elsevier Science.

Copyright © 2003, Elsevier Science (USA).

 Recognizing the importance of preserving what has been written, Elsevier Science prints its books on acid-free paper whenever possible.

Library of Congress Cataloging-in-Publication Data
Yeschke, Charles L.
    The art of investigative interviewing : a human approach to testimonial evidence / Charles L. Yeschke.—2nd ed.
      p. cm.
    Includes bibliographical references and index.
    ISBN 0-7506-7595-0 (pbk. : alk. paper)
    1. Interviewing in law enforcement. 2. Police questioning.
  I. Title.
  HV8073 .Y475 2002
  363.25′4—dc21   2002066615

British Library Cataloguing-in-Publication Data
A catalogue record for this book is available from the British Library.

The publisher offers special discounts on bulk orders of this book.
For information, please contact:
Manager of Special Sales
Elsevier Science
200 Wheeler Road
Burlington, MA 01803
Tel: 781-313-4700
Fax: 781-313-4882

For information on all Butterworth–Heinemann publications available, contact our World Wide Web home page at: http://www.bh.com.

10 9 8 7 6 5 4 3 2 1

Printed in the United States of America

Dedicated to the men and women who participated in the rescue efforts on September 11, 2001, in New York, USA.

Contents

3   Preparing for the Interview   35

4   Evidence   47

10 Setting, Location, Intensity, and Approach in the Interview   141

Mission Statement

It is my personal goal to encourage each state to mandate specific training for all members of the criminal justice system in the dynamics of human communication as it relates to investigative interviewing.

Introduction

This book was written for everyone who uses investigative interviewing on the job. It is intended to assist interviewers who, with self-appreciation, vision, purpose, and dedication, can commit themselves to the highest professional standards and thus contribute to the advancement of democracy.

Interviewers who use psychological tactics such as those discussed in this book tend to be less harsh, less vulnerable to criticism, more cognitive, more subjective, and more intuitive than interviewers who use coercive tactics. The use of coercive tactics is not only offensive, but also generally illegal. There is no justification for treating all interviewees as though they were guilty. Certainly, there is a time to confront the bad guy, but even then, nasty, abusive treatment is out of place. No matter what the situation, humane tactics are always best.

Interviewing is a complex process that sometimes meets with opposition. Interviewees might believe that the interview invades their privacy, deprives them of their Fifth Amendment rights, and is an unwarranted penetration of their secrets. In reality, the evaluation of truth or deception is a human diagnostic process which, when skillfully accomplished, is legal, subtle, and a vital part of human communication.

By unobtrusively directing the interview, proficient investigators decide when to talk and when to remain silent, all the while looking for, listening for, and sensing possible signs of deception. Signs of deception are indications that a person is holding back or covering up information that is vital to the investigation.

A friendly tone expresses positive feelings. It is essential to set a positive tone within the first four minutes of every interview to aid in gaining truthful information. If one interviewee is treated badly, other interviewees who hear about it may refuse to be interviewed for fear of how they will be treated, or they may become resentful and reluctant to help in the investigation.

Law enforcement officers are on the front lines safeguarding society. As part of the criminal justice team, they must be trained to collect effective testimonial evidence to be used in the fight against crime. If law enforcement officers and other members of the criminal justice system are properly instructed and learn what is expected of them, they will do a credible job. I'm convinced that behavior is learned. Therefore, let's go beyond the mandated topics and teach how to interact more effectively with other human beings on a professional level.

Interviewing, interrogating, human interaction, and communication are vital topics in the collection of testimonial evidence. Yet, many police academies erroneously assume that recruits will learn interviewing techniques while studying other topics. When the topic *is* taught, the training focuses on legally mandated topics thought to prepare recruits to serve and protect. We have no innate ability to conduct affective, effective, and proficient interviews. We are no more born with the skills to collect testimonial evidence than we are born with the innate ability to handle firearms properly or to provide first aid. It is time to teach new recruits as much about using finesse as they learn about using force.

Clearly, law enforcement officers at all levels have the professional responsibility to learn how to interact with other human beings using subtle communication skills. In this book, I encourage personal research and study, which are indispensable to comprehensive knowledge. All members of the criminal justice team can benefit from a greater comprehension of proper interviewing techniques. There is no exact blueprint for these techniques, although we are gradually formulating guidelines. We owe a debt to leaders like the late John E. Reid who, through personal example, showed us how to uncover the truth without using coercion. Those who have been exposed to his knowledge are better for it. On the job with both the CIA and the FBI, I have adapted Reid's technique to real-world situations to form my own process, which I believe advances what Reid taught me.

Ethical Standards and Practices

Over millions of years, through the intricate processes of evolution, the human being was created. Along with a unique ability to think about personal actions and the origins, value, and results of those actions, we retained ancestral instincts that helped us survive. One of those instincts is aggression. The most aggressive early humans became the most fit of the species and were the ones to survive. Though aggression seems at times to be the ultimate evil, it does serve a purpose. Many people today believe that through self-awareness and the search for truth, human beings can learn to channel their aggressive instincts in productive ways to become humane, moral creatures living in a truly good world.

GOOD AND EVIL

The essence of goodness is to preserve life, to promote happiness, and to help people achieve their goals. To early human beings, goodness meant survival. Evil, however, was more complex; it probably meant harm, fear of the unknown, the magical and dangerous darkness. When human beings began to record their feelings, they talked of this basic evil. As human sophistication increased, our conceptions of good and evil also became more complex. Humans moved far beyond merely valuing their own lives; they became concerned with the kinds of lives they led. Which values were good ones? How did they know when they were evil? Society told them, and different societies offered different answers.

For centuries, westerners looked upon themselves as innately evil. In the sixteenth and seventeenth centuries, superstitious concepts of evil ran wild, and witch-hunting arose—a natural outcome when evil could be defined by one's fears and resentments of others. Philosophers of the eighteenth century believed that human beings begin life as good and innocent creatures but are doomed to corruption by society. The nineteenth-century Victorians believed that science and progress, hand in hand with God, would bring people to a realizable state of perfection. Of course, whether humans are considered essentially good or essentially evil is academic in the everyday world.

Values

Every society has embraced moral codes and has formulated rules of conduct. The rules a society chooses are dependent on the goals of that society and its leaders. By making rules, societies define evil, and such official definitions vary greatly among different societies. Today, the actions and values of an individual are guided not only by the imposed laws of church and state, but also by the all-pervasive arena of public opinion.

In addition to society, religion, and public opinion, we derive our values from other, more personal, sources. Children learn values from parents who lay down the law and act as examples of conduct and from teachers who impart more than facts to their students. Sometimes the moral lessons are straightforward and undisguised, but often they are more subtle, taught by implication and example.

Despite all the guidelines, the laws, the shining examples, and the taboos, we all reach a stage where we look to ourselves for answers and decide what we believe and where we stand. What should we do if society, religion, or public opinion dictates one thing and our conscience another? Judged by our deeds, we must take responsibility for our own acts. In 1842, the poet Alfred Lord Tennyson (1809–1892) asked, "Ah, when shall all men's good be each man's rule, and universal peace lie like a shaft of light across the land?" For "all men's good" to be "each man's rule," we must act with reason, for reason is our unique advantage as human beings. We must learn to redirect our aggression so that we do not destroy our fellow beings and the world in which we live.

Aggression can be bent to useful purposes—to explore, to construct, and to compete without hostility. If we wish to remain human, we must acknowledge our animal heritage and use it. Only by accepting and exploring our instincts will we truly understand our values and ourselves. Even then, however, each of us will have to rely on our own conscience. If we wish to stand outside the general laws, to act on our personal values, to define our own good and evil, we must know why we do so. In choosing this hardest path of all, we cannot shift responsibility from ourselves. We must believe in what we do and be ready for the consequences of rebellion.

THE FOUNDATION OF ETHICS

Ethics is the inherent inner voice, the source of self-control in the absence of external compulsion. I think that ethics can be defined as knowing the difference between what is the right thing to do and what you have a right to do. Ethics can be said to be based upon the Golden Rule: "Do to others as you would have them do to you." Ethical behavior is judged by the way we act, the values that motivate us, the policies we have adopted, and the goals we seek to achieve. Every organization has an ethics strategy, whether explicit or implied. Each needs a set of ethics policies and procedures to describe how that strategy is to be implemented and how the organization's ethics goals are to be achieved. In the absence of policy, procedures, or precedents, ethical effectiveness is based upon organizational values that provide direction and consistency in decision making.

In their article, "Doing the Right Thing," H. B. Karp and Bob Abramms (1992) make a number of good points about ethics that can be applied to investigative interviewing:

- The main problem in dealing with ethics is that there is no universal definition, no clear objectives, and no agreement on appropriate behaviors. The only ethics that are realistic and worth supporting are situational ethics; what is occurring at any given point determines what actions are effective, appropriate, and ethical.
- Values define who you are. All ethical decisions are determined by values that are clear and uncompromising statements about what is critically important. In organizations, clear values drive mission statements, strategic plans, and effective, results-oriented behavior.
- Ethics come into play when external pressures force someone to act in a manner that is not consistent with his or her values. Only actions can be judged to be ethical or unethical. Ethics do not define what is acceptable about an action as much as they define what is not acceptable.
- Ethics provide a set of guidelines that outlines what constitutes appropriate behavior. Once a clearly stated code of ethics is developed and made public, individuals are responsible for their own actions. The code of ethics supports the concept of dignity as the central element that drives human interaction in the workplace. Most organizational codes of ethics clearly demand that people treat each other with respect. When we show consideration to others, we are indicating that we hold them in high regard.
- A code of ethics provides a commonly held set of guidelines that will provide a consistent, value-driven basis for

judging what is right or wrong in any given situation and establishes the outer limits of acceptable behavior.

- If a new code of ethics is truly going to be operational, people have to have an opportunity to see where the ethics originate, what purpose they serve, and how they relate to each individual.

ETHICAL LEADERSHIP

Members of an organization look to their leaders for ethical guidance. Leaders must clearly define what is right and what is wrong, telling subordinates in person what behavior is expected and what will not be tolerated. Everyone must know where they stand. Once the organization has set the ethical line, it must reward good behavior and act decisively when moral and ethical lapses occur. Edward Petry, Center for Business Ethics at Bentley College, Waltham, MA, notes in the article "Have We Lost Our Moral Compass?," "Just having an ethics policy isn't always enough. It is meaningless if not reinforced with training and communication. More telling is the hidden language of ethics. It is the accumulated informal knowledge about what is rewarded and what is punished. It is not always in sync with what's said publicly, but it's far closer to reality" (1990).

It is essential to have a written code of conduct that clearly states that dishonesty is not acceptable. It is important that this code of conduct be created from the bottom up, with input from employees at all levels. Members of the organization must see the agreement between what they are being asked to do for the organization and their values—what they personally believe is right, fair, and good. There must be a process in place that allows employees at all levels to communicate up the chain of command without fear of reprisal.

Leaders at the highest levels of the organization must clearly demonstrate their commitment to ethical behavior through their actions as well as their words. Stating an uncompromising dedication to ethics is not enough; leaders must not only talk about ethics, but also live it. They must bring respect and compassion to their management of people, providing employees with maximum opportunities to reach their highest potentials by treating them fairly, honestly, and supportively.

ETHICS FOR LAW ENFORCEMENT PROFESSIONALS

Every profession has gone through a period of development in which society questions the qualifications of the profession's members. No group can claim to be a profession until its members meet the highest standards of education, training, and experience. The professional must be regulated by laws so that society can feel confident of receiving competent, reliable services.

Each profession should take the initiative to adopt a code of ethics that is particular to the specific services it renders to society. Legislative law can go only so far in setting standards, and then the profession itself must take over, regulating its members with semijudicial procedures governing techniques and methods of service. Policies and procedures are the vehicles that an organization uses to communicate expectations and requirements to its employees. These guidelines provide an effective supplement to individual judgment. A code of ethics turns a specialty into a profession. Without their ethical codes, the legal and medical professions would not retain their high status in our society.

Some professionals, such as law enforcement officers, have an awesome responsibility: Their actions affect the life, liberty, and happiness of the individual members of society. The principal objective of ethical law enforcement professionals is to render service to society with full respect for the dignity of all in the determination of the truth. Confidence in the law enforcement professional is partly created through a public acknowledgment of the professional's integrity, education, and experience. Professionals should observe all statutes of society, should uphold the dignity and honor of the profession, and should accept its self-imposed disciplines. They should expose, without hesitation, the illegal or unethical conduct of fellow members of the profession. The law enforcement profession should safeguard the public and itself against officers who are deficient in moral character or professional competence.

Professional Integrity

The public must have confidence in the law enforcement professional's integrity and high professional standards. Law enforcement professionals must not jeopardize their integrity by personal, political, or financial associations that would improperly influence or interfere with an investigation. They should not allow the particular conditions or circumstances of an investigation to impair the free and complete exercise of their judgment and skill. Professionals will be held responsible for their acts and must be prepared to defend their professional behavior.

Criminal investigations must be conducted in a professional atmosphere in which no one tampers with evidence and no one physically or psychologically compels an innocent person to confess. Criminal investigators should practice a method of evidence collection instituted upon a diagnostic technique, and they should not professionally endorse anyone who does not. By diagnostic, I mean that the investigative search should include several avenues or procedures such as interviews, collection of real and documentary evidence, surveillance, and so forth.

The law enforcement professional's report should be a clear, concise summary of what transpired during the investigation and should record all pertinent information. All professionals should strive diligently and continually to improve their communication skills. They should be eager to advance the status of their profession by sharing their professional knowledge with their colleagues. The improvement of law enforcement standards and techniques is the direct responsibility of each member of the profession.

A SAMPLE CODE OF ETHICS FOR LAW ENFORCEMENT PROFESSIONALS

Reputable law enforcement professionals cannot claim to be perfect—they are, after all, human—but they can hold themselves to high ethical standards. I suggest that all members of the profession pledge themselves to some form of the following code of ethics:

- To verify the truth fairly, impartially, and objectively.
- To make no false statements and claims regarding personal qualifications.
- To maintain the highest standards of moral, ethical, and professional conduct.
- To be governed by laws of equity and justice in the performance of all functions.
- To respect the inherent dignity of all people.
- To be just, fair, and impartial with each individual, irrespective of social, political, racial, ethnic, or religious considerations, economic status, or physical characteristics.
- To discharge professional duties and obligations with independence, dignity, and self-respect.
- To keep all decisions and reports scrupulously free from any personal, financial, political, fraternal, social, or improper influence.
- To refrain from false or misleading reporting.
- To accept no illegal or improper remuneration for services rendered.
- To refrain from representing competing or conflicting interests when such representation is, or gives the appearance of being, unethical.

- To refrain from slanderous or libelous public criticism of the law enforcement profession or its membership, recognizing that the welfare and advancement of the profession and society supersede personal desires and ambitions.
- To recommend and accept for membership in the profession those who strive in every way to be a credit to the profession.
- To support the purposes and objectives of the profession.

Principles of Practice

Principles of practice are intended to aid professionals individually and collectively in maintaining a high level of ethical conduct. They are not laws, but standards by which all professionals may determine the appropriateness of their conduct when interacting with their peers, with members of allied professions, and with the general public.

Ethical standards are statements that represent the objectives toward which every law enforcement officer and private investigator should strive. The principles of practice can be consulted for guidance in specific situations. They help professionals meet their ethical objectives and are vital to a clear interpretation of the code of ethics.

To ensure a clear understanding of their obligations and to protect the welfare of the public, I propose that law enforcement professionals agree to abide by the following principles of practice:

- To refuse to conduct an inquiry when there is reason to believe that it is intended to circumvent or defy the law.
- To never knowingly submit or permit subordinates to submit a misleading or false report.

- To never solicit or accept fees, gratuities, or gifts that are provided to falsify or influence an inquiry.
- To respect the rights and dignity of all people.
- To avoid any demeanor, pose, duress, artifice, or device that would tend to induce a false information during an inquiry.
- To refuse to release to any unauthorized person information obtained during an inquiry.

These principles of practice establish minimal guidelines for the performance of professional activities. Conduct and practices that are not specifically stated herein but are detrimental to or discrediting to the law enforcement profession or its members should not be condoned.

CANONS OF ETHICS OF THE CALIFORNIA PEACE OFFICERS' ASSOCIATION

In its nine canons, the code of ethics of the California Peace Officers' Association enumerates the standards of professional conduct expected of its members in their relationship with the public, the criminal justice system, and the profession.

The Canons of Ethics

1. Peace Officers shall uphold the Constitution of the United States, the State Constitution and all laws enacted or established pursuant to legally constituted authority.
2. Peace Officers shall be aware of and shall use proper and ethical procedures in discharging their official duties and responsibilities.
3. Peace Officers shall regard the discharge of their duties as a public trust and shall recognize their responsibilities to the people whom they are sworn to protect and serve.

4. Peace Officers will so conduct their public and private life that they exemplify the high standards of integrity, trust, and morality demanded of a member of the peace officer profession.
5. Peace Officers shall recognize that our society holds the freedom of the individual as a paramount precept, which shall not be infringed upon without just, legal, and necessary cause.
6. Peace Officers shall assist in maintaining the integrity and competence of the peace officer profession.
7. Peace Officers shall cooperate with other officials and organizations that are using legal and ethical means to achieve the goals and objectives of the peace officer profession.
8. Peace Officers shall not compromise their integrity, nor that of their agency or profession, by accepting, giving or soliciting any gratuity.
9. Peace Officers shall observe the confidentiality of information available to them through any source, as it relates to the peace officer profession.

ETHICAL AND UNETHICAL INTERVIEWING

Throughout recorded history, one of the great problems we have faced has been the development of a system by which truth may be made known. Solutions to this problem have ranged from such extremes as the torture chambers of the middle ages to the unhesitating acceptance of the word of a gentleman in the eighteenth century. Neither extreme meets the requirements of today. We respect human dignity too much to permit physical and psychological abuse of an individual in the search for truth. Yet we recognize that our enemies will lie without hesitation, even under oath, if this will further their aims. The truth can be determined only after the evidence has been collected and analyzed. The public should not be misled into thinking that this is an automatic process. Investigative interviewers should use only the best means available on behalf of society to collect and preserve evidence.

The tactics suggested in this book to encourage the cooperation of interviewees are ethical, as defined in this chapter. This book is partly intended to counteract the often illegal coercive tactics of the past and to promote perceptive interviewing. I consider the following behaviors to be unethical:

- Using interrogation tactics instead of interviewing tactics.
- Treating each interviewee as though culpable, with little or no regard for the destructive public relations and psychological damage inflicted upon interviewees who are blameless.
- Making threats.
- Making illegal promises.
- Using coercion.
- Using duress.
- Using force or the threat of force.
- Employing ruthless methods.
- Falsely imprisoning the interviewee.
- Not respecting the interviewee.
- Not maintaining the interviewee's dignity.

These and similar tactics have been used in the past in interviews with victims and witnesses as well as suspects. It is time for change. It is time that those involved in investigative interviewing be specifically taught what is ethical and what is unethical, beyond what is legal and what is illegal.

REVIEW QUESTIONS

1. Is there any advantage in having aggressive instincts? Explain.

2. How do we learn our personal values?

3. Why must we take responsibility for our acts?

4. What is the Golden Rule, and how does it apply to ethics?

5. Do you agree that values define who you are? Explain.

6. What is the only thing that can ever be judged ethical or unethical?

7. What do most organizational codes of ethics demand?

8. Why is it important to have a written code of conduct?

9. What is the hidden language of ethics, and how can it support an organization's ethics goals?

10. What are the characteristics of a profession?

11. What is the principal objective of ethical law enforcement professionals?

12. Why must law enforcement professionals safeguard their personal integrity? How can this be done?

13. List three ethical guidelines that might appear in a code of ethics.

14. Which of the principles of practice do you consider to be the most important? Why?

15. List three interviewing tactics that you believe to be unethical, and explain why.

2

Human Needs and Deception in the Interview

By comprehending human needs, the investigator may anticipate the basic motivation of the culpable individual who is trying to rationalize and save face through deceptive tactics.

HUMAN NEEDS

Consider the human needs of interview participants! The effective interviewer sets the stage for eliciting accurate information by knowing, accepting, and attempting to satisfy the emotional needs that motivate all human activity.

Universal Human Needs

Underneath differences of culture, people everywhere are the same. "Humans are all equipped with the same emotional repertoire, the same basic needs, the same basic defenses" (Bennis et al. 1973, p. 93). Interview participants, like everyone else, are taught to be perceptive and considerate; to express themselves through their self-esteem; to have pride, honor, and dignity; to use tact; and to exhibit a certain amount of poise. In addition, they are motivated by the same basic needs as everyone else. Although we are all endowed with the same basic qualities and needs, it is how we develop those qualities and satisfy those needs that makes us unique.

I believe that crimes are committed to satisfy three basic interpersonal needs. In one form or another, these three needs often lie at the core of the criminal personality (Bennis et al. 1973, pp. 16, 48, 61).

- *Control:* The need for security. We all share a driving need to control and dominate our environment (*Productivity and the Self-Fulfilling Prophecy* 1975).
- *Belonging:* The feeling of inclusion and affiliation. This need encompasses the desire for recognition and social approval, fair treatment and a chance for advancement, prestige, and a sense of accomplishment.
- *Intimacy:* The need for love, affection, understanding, and approval; the desire for meaningful relationships with others. We all want to feel that other people accept our weaknesses and recognize our strengths.

Most people maintain the illusion of being independent, reasonable, and clear-thinking; they do not want to appear foolish (Berg and Bass 1961, p. 247). Their temperamental disposition is subtle and imperceptible, even unconscious. There is only a thin line between what they are and what they want (Bennis et al. 1973, p. 12). Interviewees who have been victimized may feel uncomfortable, embarrassed, and distressful. They don't want to admit that they have lost control in any way or that they were taken advantage of (Bennis et al. 1973, p. 195).

Self-Image and Esteem

It has been said that our greatest fear is not of dying, but of feeling unfit to live. The self is a composite of what we think, feel, believe, want, and worry about. From these subjective components we construct a self-image, and we think of ourselves as unique. Interviewees, like everyone else, treasure their sense of self. They will protect and enhance their self-image in any way they can.

Self-esteem, which is closely tied to self-image, is worth to the self; it encompasses the need for achievement, mastery, dignity, independence, and freedom. Maintaining self-esteem, or "saving face," is a central need of interview participants. Interviewees will act defensively to avoid being humiliated in front of others (Bennis et al. 1973, p. 298). Proper interview planning prevents interviewees from being made to look foolish in front of friends or associates. Negotiate with interviewees so that the interview process will not cause them too much emotional "pain" (Nierenberg 1968, p. 9). When interviewees feel that they will not totally lose face by cooperating, the interview will be a much more bearable event.

Esteem, on the other hand, consists of worth in the eyes of others—colleagues, peers, subordinates, and superiors. It is tied not only to the position one occupies, but more particularly to the personal qualities of contribution, expertise, and warmth. Esteem from others includes the desire for attention, recognition, prestige, and power. Esteem is gained from others by showing that you know what you are doing, are using technical and practical applications of knowledge, and care what happens to other people (Bowers 1976).

Like you, interviewees don't want to feel rejected and excluded (Kahn and Cannell 1957). They don't want to be thought ignorant, uninformed, or indecisive. It is only when they feel accepted by others that interviewees tend to comply (Woody and Woody 1972, p. 140). Interviewees may be reluctant to change their story to be more truthful for fear of looking bad. Hence, always give them the opportunity to provide a fresh, more accurate story. They need support to modify or elaborate on facts they have presented. My experience indicates that once having made a general conclusion, a witness is not likely to report individual facts inconsistent with that conclusion.

Satisfaction of Needs

"It is human nature to think wisely and act foolishly."

—*Anatole France*

Humans function mostly on feelings and not logic. Human behavior may at first appear haphazard because it is made up of habits, instincts, intelligence, and learning; these elements overlap and are not clear-cut (Nierenberg 1968, p. 35). The fundamentals of human personality are needs, emotions, thinking, and the ability to relate thoughts and feelings. Our actions are a result and composite of all of these elements.

But most of all, it is the satisfaction of essential and predictable needs that motivates every type of human behavior. Individuals try to satisfy their needs by maintaining physical comfort, avoiding the unsafe, attempting to gain understanding, detesting anonymity, desiring to be free from boredom, fearing the unknown, and hating disorder. Underlying every interview action is a desire to satisfy basic human needs (Nirenberg 1963, p. 22). Because social needs are comparatively unsatisfied, they have become a primary motivator for behavior. Interviewees desperately seek approval and reassurance that they are in control and are worthy. Participants who feel threatened, inferior, or ridiculous will try to increase feelings of security, acceptance, and self-regard. Many human needs can be fulfilled through conversation. Everyone experiences feelings of inferiority from time to time. You may succeed in gaining the cooperation of interviewees if you nourish them with feelings of security, friendship, and dignity and encourage them as they strive to satisfy their needs.

As we strive, directly or indirectly, to satisfy our needs, we have urges to behave in ways that will help or hinder our striving. The psychiatrist William C. Menninger states, "The problem is one of achieving a balance between what we want and what we get. We all want things, but the more adult among us learn to master our frustrations and to recognize that we cannot have what we want when we want it. To be truly adult and efficient persons, we have to learn to find satisfaction in daily life" (1953, p. 26). Complications may develop as we seek to satisfy our needs. Either we modify our behavior to overcome the obstacles that are blocking the satisfaction of our needs, or we become frustrated at our failures. Frustration may provoke the emotional reactions of aggression, regression, and fixation as well as assorted defense mechanisms.

Refusal to Cooperate

Wherever we go, we believe we have the right not to be touched, the right not to be dragged into conversation with a stranger, and the right to privacy. The assumption of these universal rights influences how interviewees expect to be treated in an investigation (Davis 1975, p. 180). Interviewees frequently comment, "I don't want to get involved." Although this statement might reflect a desire to protect themselves, occasionally it also means that they want to protect another person. Revealing someone else's self is almost as difficult as revealing your own.

The effort to gain the interviewee's cooperation can sometimes be frustrating. Interviewees might refuse to become involved in an investigation because they fear callous or indifferent treatment from legal authorities, fear of reprisal from the guilty party or others, inconvenience and financial loss, and confusion over legal proceedings. To some interviewees, court appearances entail an unnecessary burden on their time and energy.

Fear of Self-Disclosure

You get to know other people intimately when they reveal to you their innermost thoughts, feelings, and desires (Bennis et al. 1973, p. 541). However, people are reluctant to share their inner self with strangers and will do what they can to avoid self-disclosure in an interview (Bennis et al. 1973, p. 542). People regard their assumptions and conclusions as sensible and valid, tending to adhere dogmatically to their chosen ways (Berg and Bass 1961, p. 144). Thus interviewees may be defensive and make excuses for their actions (Wicks and Josephs 1972). To counter this fear, the investigator can, if emotionally strong, reveal some life experience that expresses personal vulnerabilities. Such action shows the interviewer's humanness and approachability. Self-disclosure is scary to us all.

Fear of Harming Others

Some interviewees act as a stand-in for someone else who is not even present, trying to maintain that person's self-image (Bennis et al. 1973, p. 181). Knowing the inner self of someone else is a sacred trust, so interviewees may hesitate to reveal what they know about others. Even when interviewees feel a sense of civic duty to cooperate with an investigation, they may be reluctant to provide information that could cause harm to come to another. Many recall the admonition, "Judge not, lest ye be judged." Hence, interviewing someone about a third party's actions can be extremely difficult. You can help the interviewee overcome his or her reservations by suggesting that truthful cooperation will best serve the third party's interest despite any immediate danger.

The Interviewer's Task

Success in influencing the behavior of interviewees—in convincing them to answer questions honestly—begins with your attempt to understand and, to some extent, satisfy the needs underlying their behavior. The anticipation and satisfaction of needs is central to successful interviewing. If you fail to anticipate the interviewee's needs, tension will develop, and unless the interviewee's basic needs are fulfilled, the interview will be little more than a waste of time. We need to control or maintain a satisfactory relationship with other people with respect to power and influence. The investigator's understanding of human nature, preparation, and strategy combine to help satisfy the interviewee's needs (Nierenberg 1968). By actively listening, the investigator exhibits understanding and acceptance of the interviewee's needs. By attempting to gain a deeper understanding of the interviewee's needs, the investigator uncovers possible evasiveness and distress.

Pressures, loyalties, obligations, needs, and restrictions frequently cause interviewees to be uncomfortable and not relaxed mentally. To gain their cooperation requires kindness and consideration of their position in life, their needs, and their privacy (Bowers 1976). Some interviewees feel abandoned. Their vulnerability may have a disruptive effect on their cooperation. Although interviewers cannot realistically take the place of neighbors and close kin to reduce the interviewee's sense of abandonment, they can exhibit human warmth and thereby psychologically comfort them enough to encourage temporary compliance.

Responding to Anger

Many people have a real problem with anger; others claim that they never feel it. Some people, in the midst of rage, even deny that they are angry. If a person's sense of safety, acceptance, or effectiveness is shaken, one resulting emotion will be anger (Cavanagh 1979). You might well encounter anger in the interview room, from both the truthful and the deceptive. Honest interviewees might become angry because of inconvenience, the loss of face, or other reasons. You can quell their anger by remaining calm and in control. On the other hand, deceptive interviewees may feign anger as a defensive ploy to hide their deception. They will often not be calmed down. Their intent is to put you on the defensive and to make it appear that your further effort is hopeless.

With interviewees exhibiting anger or anxiety, remain controlled, understanding, and nonjudgmental. If the interviewee verbally attacks you, avoid retaliation. If challenged into a defensive stance, think clearly and remain objective. Nothing positive is accomplished by taking up their challenge. Take pride in your emotional control even when faced with insults or threats that would cause other people to retaliate (Nirenberg 1963). An interview is more of a marathon than a sprint. Although you may think it necessary to win, the main challenge is to just stay in there. The culpable will likely lose the race for themselves with your help, so to speak.

The Interviewer's Needs

Experienced interviewers learn to keep their own needs in check during an investigation. Investigators who try to fulfill egocentric, personal, or childish needs in an interview may become frustrated; they may act out personal tensions by misusing their authority (Bennis et al. 1973, p. 201). Freud stated, "Aggressiveness, held back, seems to involve grave injury. It really seems as though it is necessary for us to destroy some things or person in order not to destroy ourselves, in order to guard against the impulse of self-destruction" (Yeschke, 1993, p. 49). We are not far removed from our primitive nature. The potential for destructiveness goes with a position of authority. Given authority, some individuals become destructive in ways and at times that are not helpful to society.

Whatever your tactics, be sure they are ethical—that is, based on respect for the interviewee's rights. The civilized and compassionate treatment of victims, witnesses, and suspects is necessary if you are to obtain truthful cooperation. Do not use coercion, intimidation, threats, promises, or duress to force a confession; such tactics are self-defeating and inappropriate as well as illegal. Intimidation reaps only resentment, not truthful cooperation. Although the real-world objective of forensic interviewing is often the swift and sure punishment of wrongdoers, there is no reason to treat interviewees abusively.

When the self-image and self-esteem of interview participants are at stake and basic human needs require fulfillment, pressure results. Police officers, in particular, are under intense stress as they routinely face the worst of humanity, witness terrible events, and make difficult decisions (Freeman 1942). Overstimulation of the body's autonomic nervous system, which governs involuntary actions, routinely adds to distress, particularly when there is no way to vent built-up pressure. When the investigation becomes intense, stressful enough to cause emotional involvement, proficient interviewers try to remain detached.

DECEPTION

> "The essence of lying is in deception, not in words. A lie may be told by silence, by equivocation, by the accent on a syllable, by a glance of the eyes attaching a peculiar significance to a sentence, and all these kinds of lies are worse and baser by many degrees than a lie plainly worded."
>
> —*John Ruskin*

Before we explore deception, let's establish some criteria for credibility. The credibility of interviewees is based on their truthfulness and believability, and it is related to their observation skills and accuracy in reporting. Here are five possible tests of interviewee credibility:

1. Was the interviewee present and aware during the incident? Presence includes more than being there physically. The interviewee might have been "present" by means of a telephone or binoculars, for example. Awareness relates to age and intelligence. An adult may be able to describe the chain of events leading to an assault; a child may comprehend only that "Daddy hit Mommy."
2. Was the interviewee attentive during the incident? The interviewer must distinguish the interviewee's actual experience from his or her feelings about what was observed.
3. How well developed are the interviewee's powers of observation?
4. Can the interviewee relate the facts briefly, correctly, and clearly without showing signs of emotional disturbance?

5. Does the interviewer's nonverbal behavior signal deception?

Truthfulness is signaled by an acute memory, a perceptive recounting of facts, and a flowing narration. Truthful interviewees display a consistent recollection of details and attempt to dig up related specifics, often offering more information than they are asked for. With encouragement, they remember facts they thought they had forgotten. They will allow the interviewer to see their mental wheels moving in search of additional details. With the truthful, you might witness a furrowed brow, squinted eyes, and a contemplative silence. They are open and relaxed in their manner of speech, though they may be somewhat uneasy. In addition, they clearly explain the sequence of events, wanting to be correct.

⁓ Deception is the intentional act of concealing or distorting the truth for the purpose of misleading. Interviewees deceive when they deliberately hide from the interviewer what they saw or what they did, and why.

Convincing liars are often self-assured and cunning. They can be difficult to identify because their comments are never too strong, too defensive, or out of context. Their motivation to lie is rarely based on anger or hostility; that would weaken the basis of their confidence. If they are trying to help someone by lying, they will be at ease, and their comments will sound natural. Because they have rationalized their lying, they maintain both confidence and peace of mind, suffering no pangs of conscience. Conscience is the internal sense of what is right and wrong that governs a person's thoughts and actions, urging him or her to do the right thing. Conscience is expressed through behavior.

Warning Signs of Deception

"He that has eyes to see and ears to hear may convince himself that no mortal can keep a secret. If his lips are silent, he chatters with his fingertips; betrayal oozes out of him at every pore."

—*Sigmund Freud (as quoted in Davis, 1975)*

While some interviewees are capable of maintaining astonishingly good control of both verbal and nonverbal responses to questioning, most others display telltale signs of deception. Some can't stand the tension of even trying to deceive, and they readily admit the truth (Binder and Price 1977, p. 118). As children, most people were taught the same set of social norms. They learned to treat strangers courteously, to behave hospitably toward visitors, to answer when spoken to, to tell the truth, and to obey the reasonable requests of authorities. All things being equal, people prefer to answer rather than to remain silent, and to tell the truth rather than to fabricate. Violating these social norms causes most interviewees stress, and they display this stress through their verbal responses, nonverbal behavior, and physiological reactions during the interview.

Deceptive interviewees use language to mask their lies. They avoid eye-to-eye contact as they talk around relevant topics, often offering seemingly useless and irrelevant comments. The deceptive characteristically answer questions in a limited manner without volunteering additional data. They take a protected stance, knowing that the less they say, the less likely it is that they will be caught in a lie. Although they smile and look somewhat composed, their tone of voice and physical actions appear unnatural to a skilled interviewer.

More than a gut feeling, or intuition, is required to detect deception. It helps to be so familiar with the verbal and nonverbal behaviors that signal deception that you note them automatically. You should continually be alert for inconsistent, evasive responses punctuated by nonverbal signals that indicate imbalance. To me, imbalance is reflected in interviewee unevenness of emphasis, verbally and nonverbally. It is a state of disharmony or inability to function in proportion to the situation. Social scientists have found that vocal intonation, timing, silence, body positioning, facial expression, and eye movement may confirm, obscure, or contradict spoken words. Although there is no failsafe method of detecting deception in an interviewee, certain verbal, nonverbal, and physiological signs have generally been reliable. These indicators of probable deception are discussed below.

When you suspect that an interviewee is being less than truthful, do not immediately announce your suspicion. Instead, go on with your questioning, and continue to note the verbal and nonverbal signs of deception. Challenging the interviewee's veracity before you have accumulated sufficient data on which to make a conclusive decision may hinder the progress of the interview.

Verbal Signs

Only a skilled actor can lie in a believable way—and then with only a very limited expression of the facts. The deceptive offer convoluted explanations or sophisticated evasions. They may present a complex, tangled, or confused explanation in response to your question, or they may try to dodge the question altogether. Their answers are general in nature and broad in content. Their desire, apparently, is to say as little as possible while hiding in their self-made emotional shelter. They may think that if they are silent and motionless, no one will guess they are hiding the truth. They seem to take comfort in their lack of spontaneity, and they think they are safe and secure as they try not to be noticed.

A lack of clear thinking may signal deception and evasiveness. When interviewees express themselves in a calculated, dissociated, or awkward manner rather than in a smooth, flowing way, something, somewhere, is not altogether right. The deceptive tend to assert that they don't remember, while truthful interviewees tend not to say this. A person who wants to hide relevant information must make a conscious effort to keep the truth submerged. That effort requires contemplation, intention, and planning, all of which may happen in a brief moment, followed by a "memory lapse." The deceptive answer more evasively than the truthful. They use phrases like "I would deny that allegation" and "I can't tell you much about that." They may attempt to distract the interviewer with inappropriate friendliness, compliments, or seductive behavior.

When interviewees begin with the words "To be honest," "To tell the truth," "Frankly," or "Honestly," they most likely do *not* intend to be frank or honest. Interviewees who express objections rather than denials when questioned are probably not being completely truthful. Interviewees who were later shown to be lying have said the following:

- "I have plenty of money in the bank. I would have no reason to take that money."
- "I'm not the kind of person who would think of doing that."
- "I don't go around doing those kinds of things."
- "I couldn't do something like that."

The objections tend to be true, at least in part. The suspect who utters the first objection may indeed have money in the bank, but that response is not a clear denial of having stolen. Honest denials are straightforward and crystal clear: "No, I didn't steal the money."

Nonverbal Signs

Gestures, mannerisms, facial expressions, and other forms of nonverbal communication are learned throughout life; they reveal underlying personality traits, subconscious attitudes, intentions, and conflicts. The more you know about nonverbal communication, the better an interviewer you will be. Your observation of the interviewee's unintentional nonverbal cues can help you make decisions about his or her truthfulness. When interviewees twist the truth, they leave clues in their facial expressions and bodily movements. Their expressions and body language may convey internal struggles as they try to cover the outward signs of lying. A mere twitch or an effort to control such a barely perceptible movement is enough indication to warn that the interviewee's response may be a fabrication (Davis 1975, p. 25).

After answering a question dishonestly, some interviewees immediately look searchingly at your eyes and face for any nonverbal signs of your skepticism. This subconscious, questioning, wide-open look lasts only a fraction of a moment. While deceptive interviewees pretend to ponder questions, they may engage in some physical action that betrays their desire to escape from the interview—mentally if not physically. This uneasiness may manifest itself as they shuffle their feet, cross their legs, or cover their eyes. They often avoid eye contact by looking around the room or at the floor, frequently picking real or imagined lint from their clothes. In addition, they blink more often than truthful interviewees.

They may appear calm—but in a forced way. Although they smile and look composed, the deceptive often seem physically restrained. Their movements are often overly controlled and repetitive, lacking complexity and variety, not spontaneous and free moving. Interviewees who engage in rehearsed gestures, without putting their bodies into motion in a smooth, convincing manner, signal their intent to deceive. They present a false image of themselves and hope that you will accept it without question.

Physiological Signs

It is not unusual for the deceptive to exhibit symptoms of physical shock while answering questions. These symptoms include light-headedness and numbness in the extremities due to reduced blood circulation. These physiological symptoms may be a response to the interviewee's feeling of being trapped and not knowing what to do. When lying, interviewees may also exhibit physiological cues such as burping, sweating, crying, and appearing to be in a state of turmoil. Truthful individuals generally do not undergo such stress when questioned, particularly when the interviewer remains calm and restrained.

Psychological Motives for Deception

No one is forced to lie; it is a conscious decision. Deceptive interviewees might choose to hide the truth for a couple of reasons.

For some people, the interview is an exercise in survival. Telling the truth might result in a confession, and with that might come shame, embarrassment, and punishment. How interviewees evaluate the hazards in any given interview is up to the individual being questioned and depends on what they have to hide. For other people, the interview is a game. The punishment and shame associated with getting caught are not as important as matching wits with the investigator. They make it their challenge to outsmart the interviewer. Much more could be said regarding the psychological motives behind deception, but in one form or another, these motives are woven among the interviewee's efforts to satisfy basic human needs.

The Pathological Liar

Pathological liars habitually tell lies so exaggerated or bizarre that they are suggestive of mental disorder. They fabricate when it would be simpler and more convenient to tell the truth. Their stories are often complex rationalizations leading to self-vindication. Pathological liars have been fabricating stories since childhood and can be recognized by their continued performance throughout life (Cameron and Cameron 1951, pp. 206–208).

As interviewees, pathological liars are quite convincing when they say they did not just say what they actually did say. Most have the ability to refute your recall and notes pertaining to their comments. When faced with what they said only moments before, they will say something like, "Oh, no, I didn't say that!" This is when you have a reality check with yourself to see if you have lost your grip on the here and now. You know you know what they said, but you check your notes to be sure. This is not the time to enter into an I-said-you-said game with the interviewee. Be strong and restrain your inclination to do battle because you will lose in the end. After all, if you want information you can use, you can't win such a battle and expect friendly cooperation.

The Psychopathic Personality

The psychopathic personality develops along asocial and amoral lines and cannot adjust to society's standards. The psychopath is supremely selfish, living only for immediate gratification without regard for the consequences. Normal individuals often sacrifice for the possibilities of the future and show a willingness to defer certain gratifications. Psychopaths have no understanding of, and even express contempt for, the future. Dr. E. W. Cocke says this about the psychopath (1953, p. 13):

> He is always able to differentiate between right and wrong and usually is well acquainted with the requirements of society and religion, but he is absolutely unwilling to be governed by these laws. In fact, he may say that they do not concern him. The only interest which he has with laws is to see that he is not caught in their violation, and, if he is caught, to try to secure, by some trick, a minimum punishment. Thus, one of the symptoms is a complete selfishness which manifests itself in every act of the person. The only one whom he thinks of, in fact, the only individual that he completely loves, is himself, and he is surprisingly hardened to the rest of the world, including the members of his own family.

According to researcher George N. Thompson, the secondary characteristics of a psychopath are "lack . . . of discretion, judgment and wisdom, impulsiveness, peculiar ability to ingratiate himself, and inability to profit by experience" (1953, p. 42).

There is no satisfactory treatment for psychopathic personality. Psychiatrists have, so far, been unable to do any good once the psychopathic behavior pattern has been established. Neither a long term in prison nor restraint in a psychiatric hospital can affect the conduct of psychopaths. Appearing self-assured, psychopaths are often cunning and convincing liars. Their motivation is to outsmart the investigator. Yet they can be caught because, as Dr. Stanley Abrams says, "the fear of detection [still] exists and probably accounts for their reactivity" during polygraph tests (1977, p. 44). Proficient investigators consider this group challenging.

Defense Mechanisms

Most interviewees want to preserve their reputation. They strive continually to preserve their ranking among their peers by engaging in whatever action is necessary to maintain their prestige or dignity. Thus in embarrassing situations, they appreciate being allowed to save face through rationalization or projection.

Rationalization   To rationalize is to invent plausible explanations for actions (Nierenberg 1968). Interviewees, like all of us, act in accordance with their own individual rational, reasoning powers. They protect themselves with rationalizations when they hold hidden images of themselves that the facts of their status do not support (Nierenberg 1968, p. 39). Thus they use rationalization to preserve their self-image (Berg and Bass 1961, p. 252). Be sensitive to the possibility that mere involvement in an investigation might cause some interviewees to feel that they have not lived up to their personal expectations (Bennis et al. 1973, p. 274).

Everyone wants to feel capable, normal, and worthwhile compared to others. Few people are self-confident enough to be completely indifferent to insults and criticisms. They maintain their self-image by conforming to peer pressure, which can produce feelings of conflict and guilt when group behavior contradicts the dictates of their conscience. Hence interviewees will rationalize their actions, not wanting to expose their dependence on others (Berg and Bass 1961, p. 247). By accepting their rationalizations, you can help interviewees feel more confident and lessen their feelings of self-doubt. As a result, you will be more likely to gain their cooperation (Nirenberg 1963).

You can encourage interviewees to look at circumstances more optimistically (Wicks and Josephs 1972), diminishing the negative aspects of the situation through a look or a gesture, to reduce the interviewee's reluctance to cooperate. You might suggest that the interviewee's action (or lack of action) is not so unique after all and that many people have temporarily lost control (Wicks and Josephs 1972). Although you are diminishing the significance of their acts, you are not changing their overall responsibility for their actions or overlooking the effect on society and on others (Drake 1972, p. 34). Your response merely allows for the free flow of information (Bennis et al. 1973, p. 312).

You may need to help some interviewees rationalize their cooperation with the investigation. Cooperation may cause them to lose face if it cannot be justified. If low self-esteem is the price of assisting with an investigation, some interviewees will refuse.

Projection Humans try to appear reasonable to themselves and to others by doing what is proper and acceptable. Some people use the defense mechanism of projection to shift onto others the responsibilities that they have not adequately handled (Woody and Woody 1972). When they cannot live up to expectations, they blame other people or the situation itself for their behavior. As researchers have noted, "Characteristically, people look to themselves as the source of their successes and to the situation as the source for their failures" (Downs et al. 1980, p. 224). They use projection to make their behavior understandable and socially acceptable. Thus, it is always someone else's fault; it is someone else who deserves the blame (*Empathy in Police Work* 1972). Subtly assist interviewees project their blame onto others in their effort to save face.

Concluding There's Deception

The scientific method generally involves the use of inductive logic, which requires repeated observations of an experiment or of an event. From observing many different examples, scientists can draw a general conclusion (Egler 1970). Scientists also use deductive logic, reasoning from known scientific principles or rules to draw a conclusion about a specific case. The accuracy of a conclusion reached by deductive logic depends on the accuracy of the principles or rules on which it is based (Sipe 1985).

Skilled interviewers use deductive logic when reaching a conclusion about the interviewee's truthfulness. When interviewing, consider the subject's verbal and nonverbal behavior as elements of the whole. Considering the totality of the circumstances, look for a pattern that indicates truthfulness or deception.

The interviewer's tactics are based on generalizations accumulated from personal experience. Whether they work or not, generalizations give an illusion of power and are greatly cherished. Faulty, misleading generalizations can negatively influence the accuracy of the interviewer's conclusions. Therefore, judge each situation on its own merits using generalizations validated by either scientific experimentation or personal experience (Nirenberg 1963). Scientific research is sometimes subject to bias and open to serious question, so place the highest value on your own experience (Coleman 1976, p. 22).

REVIEW QUESTIONS

1. Name three basic interpersonal needs.
2. Define *esteem* and *self-esteem*.
3. How do interviewees try to protect their self-image?
4. What is the relationship between needs and human behavior?
5. What can you do to influence the interviewee's behavior?
6. Why would a person resist answering your questions about someone else?
7. How does an understanding of the interviewee's needs help you achieve your objective?
8. What is the best response to an interviewee's anger?
9. What are the four tests of interviewee credibility?
10. How do the truthful typically answer questions?
11. What is deception?

12. Why are convincing liars difficult to detect?

13. Identify several verbal, nonverbal, and physiological signs of deception.

14. What is the significance of an interviewee's responding with objections rather than denials?

15. How does the deceptive person's eye contact differ from that of the truthful person?

16. List three key characteristics of a psychopath.

17. Contrast *rationalization* and *projection.*

18. Why do people rationalize?

19. Why do pathological liars lie? Why do other people lie?

20. On what should you base your conclusion about the interviewee's truthfulness?

3

Preparing for the Interview

An archer does not become a marksman without first practicing for hours using tried-and-true procedures. Time and again, an archer will draw the bow and release the arrow so that he or she gets the feel of successful accomplishment. Hitting the pre-selected mark becomes more predictable with each draw and release. Self-efficacy is at play as arrows hit their mark.

Days, weeks, and years of practice pay off for the investigator too as he or she conducts more and more interviews. An investigator's confidence builds up over time and interviews become more fruitful. An investigator will start to notice a gradual attitude change toward interviewing and acquiring information from victims, witnesses, and suspects. As an investigator applies his or her intuition toward various assigned tasks, there is a broadening element of curiosity and flexibility flavored by imagination. These elements help build the maturing attitude and allow for greater accomplishment.

ATTITUDE

The more effective you are in collecting testimonial evidence in an interview, the more proficient you will be as an investigator. The attitude you bring to each interview is critical. A positive attitude plays a more essential role in determining your success than any procedure or technique. Your responses to interviewees will be automatic and effective if your attitude is correct.

Attitudes predispose us to behave in certain ways. Participants on both sides of the interview may have attitudes of trust or skepticism, prejudice or tolerance, toward each other. Your attitude toward interviewees determines how you treat them, which in turn influences their reaction to you. It is striking to note how sensitively interviewees react to the investigator's attitude, mood, approach, and expectations.

If the response you seek in an interview is full and open cooperation, then you must maintain a positive attitude toward each and every interviewee—even "lowlifes." Your desire to understand is crucial (Woody and Woody 1972). It is useful to maintain a calm understanding without being ruffled or shocked; be permissive in your attitude to promote cooperation (Kahn and Cannell 1957). Through active listening (see Chapter 6), you exhibit a positive, understanding attitude toward others. By having confidence in your skills and ability, you display that you are self-assured. Neighborliness will sow positive seeds of your attitude, persistence, and general determination along the investigative path. Sensing your helping, friendly attitude, interviewees will probably comply as expected. A positive attitude is always effective, no matter what your objective.

Perceptive interviewees can sense your attitude as it is expressed through the formulation and presentation of your questions and by the way you listen to the responses. They are keenly aware of verbal and nonverbal signals expressing negative attitudes. If you ridicule or degrade interviewees, you will only promote antagonism. Don't even knock the interviewee's possessions. People are proud of their things. As Shakespeare wrote, "A poor thing, but mine own."

The Components of a Positive Attitude

The personal characteristics of "warmth, empathy, acceptance, caring, liking, interest, [and] respect [toward] others" (Cameron and Cameron 1951, p. 233), along with the ability to project these qualities, will help you become a proficient interviewer. If you do not possess these characteristics, strive to attain them. Thus, "genuinely like your fellow man, be a warm, interested, caring, and involved person" (Benjamin 1974, p. 41).

You will be successful in your interviews if you incorporate three main qualities in your positive attitude:

Congruence. To be in congruence with yourself means to be aware of and comfortable with your feelings and to be able to communicate constructively with interviewees in a way that expresses your humanity. To be in congruence with the interviewee means to recognize and accept the human qualities, needs, and goals that we all share.

Unconditional positive regard. Just as a parent expresses unconditional love for a child, you should strive to display a positive regard for the interviewee without reservations or judgments. Regardless of the inquiry, and even when dealing with unsavory interviewees, treat everyone as a valuable human being. Develop a genuine liking for people, and be tolerant of human weakness. When dealing with interviewees whom you consider to be repugnant, do not show how you really feel. When your inner feelings are critical of the interviewee's behavior, put on a convincing show of acceptance of or tolerance for their behavior. This show is intended to encourage interviewees to let down their guard when talking with you. Your success is achieved by providing "warm regard for fellow human beings" despite your prejudices and shortcomings (Benjamin 1974, p. 25). Avoid condemning any behavior that conflicts with your own standards, and don't display your biases (Garrett 1972, p. 26).

Empathy. Empathy is the ability to identify with someone else, to understand their thoughts and feelings as if they were your own, and to convey this understanding to others (Woody and Woody 1972, p. 131). Pay attention as interviewees express themselves verbally and nonverbally so that you can pick up on their messages. Interviewees often express some deep emotional hurt that influenced their behavior in some way. By comprehending those hurts and putting them into your own words, you show that you are deeply tuned in, and this expresses closeness and caring.

Control your negative feelings about those with whom you come in contact during an investigation (Garrett 1972, p. 19). Even if interviewees lie to you, don't be vindictive in your comments. That's not the way to gain further information. Internally forgive the interviewee, and move on. Forgiveness requires ignoring your pride and acting unselfishly (Bennis et al. 1973, p. 140). Remind yourself that accomplishing your goal is more important than fortifying your self-esteem.

Avoid an attitude of condescension, contempt, or arrogance toward the interviewee (OSS Assessment Staff 1948, p. 16). However "bad" the interviewee has been, restrain yourself from lecturing or becoming indignant. Never allow the interviewee's mood to adversely alter your attitude or behavior. If antagonism does develop in an interview, be sure that you are not responsible for its development (Garrett 1972, p. 21). Continue as best you can to work toward gathering truthful information for a worthy goal (Bennis et al. 1973, p. 278). In all of your encounters, be a fact gatherer, not a judge. Learn the truth so that you can help resolve the matter under investigation (Wicks and Josephs 1972). Learn to be responsible for the effort, not the outcome. (This advice is especially useful for new officers.)

Attitude Change

> "The greatest revolution in our generation is the discovery that human beings, by changing the inner attitudes of their minds, can change the outer aspects of their lives."
>
> —*William James (1842–1910)*

Attitudes learned and reinforced throughout life through interactions with other people form the basis of our behavior. Attitudes are "frozen," and it is only with great effort that an "unfreezing process" takes place (Bennis et al. 1973, p. 290). Genuine attitude change is based on your predisposition and desire to change. As a professional, you can make a commitment to modify your attitudes and thus change your behavior to become a more effective interviewer. To change your attitudes, you must first change your feelings or your thinking. Authoritarianism, which breeds resentment, retaliation, and reluctance or refusal to cooperate, is largely based on prejudice (Adorno 1950). To change your authoritarian habits, look at yourself clearly and understand how your discriminatory actions affect others (Adorno 1950, p. 975).

A significant challenge is to become aware of your own strengths and limitations. The more aware you are of your good and bad characteristics as an investigator, the more likely it is that you will make changes to improve yourself. With a positive attitude, proper preparation, and adequate self-control, most interviewers can conduct productive forensic interviews (OSS Assessment Staff 1948, p. 210). If your coworkers are striving toward a positive changing of attitude, join in (Bennis et al. 1973, p. 295). The support of your associates can help you achieve the changes you desire. Discussions among small groups of peers are highly effective in influencing changes of opinion and attitude.

FLEXIBILITY

Flexibility implies a growth in the ability to shift where needed in the process of interviewing. It suggests being capable of dancing to the emotional tune played by the interviewee. The score of that tune is based on the human needs of the interviewee. Using certain steps in rhythm with the tune, the interviewer blends his or her complimentary behavior. Through the eyes of the information provider, the investigator becomes aware of the interviewee's characteristics and decides how to interact. Setting a strategic plan for each interviewee allows the investigator opportunity to gain the most from the interview. To obtain the cooperation of some interviewees, you may need to temporarily modify your methods and thinking. That is, you may have to do or say things that you might normally find objectionable. For example, if you are neutral when interacting with the interviewee, I suggest leaning for the interviewee by giving the impression that if you were in a similar circumstance, you might have done something similar to what the interviewee did, even though you know that you would never engage in that particular behavior. Treat everyone you interview—even those you suspect of involvement in the matter under investigation—with professionalism and neutrality. Your professional, calm, nonjudgmental methods signal to victims, witnesses, and suspects that they can safely trust you. Convince interviewees that you are more friend than enemy. This is how you outsmart the culpable.

Do not feel embarrassed about failing to censure those whom you feel deserve it. You do not violate your personal code of conduct by treating all interviewees with nonjudgmental acceptance. On the contrary, it is the brutal tactics of the past that do the most harm. Such methods cause useless anxiety and distress; they hurt the naive and sensitive while further alienating the sophisticated and cynical. Tactics of brutality might boost the interviewer's self-image but, in the long run, will not advance his or her professional career.

The ability to size up people and to read their basic personality type is a useful skill. Adapt your interviewing techniques to suit each interviewee. Many people interpret hurried methods and indifference as signs of insincerity. With interviewees of this type, you'll need to take your time and clearly express your interest in what they have to say. Other interviewees respond well to a businesslike attitude. To gain the trust and respect of this type of person, have facts and figures at your fingertips, and use systematic, thorough methods. Other interviewees feel a strong moral obligation to speak the truth. Overall, with interviewees who are predisposed to be cooperative and truthful, most of the methods and techniques suggested in this book will be unnecessary. As you seek to uncover the truth in an interview, be alert to—and seize—opportunities as they arise. Do not adhere rigidly to your favorite interviewing methods. Without losing sight of your objective, try several methods of questioning with uncooperative interviewees. This is where the art of interviewing enters the picture.

CURIOSITY

Curiosity is closely tied to enthusiasm or eagerness to learn. By having a generous interest to comprehend details of a situation through the eyes of the interviewee, the investigator not only sees facts more clearly but also has a chance to evaluate the interviewee.

Suspicion is a part of the investigator's job. Investigative interviews necessarily take place to uncover the truth, and you may suspect that each interviewee has some piece of the truth to reveal. You might well question the trustworthiness of everyone you encounter. After all, trusting every interviewee completely would be naive. Nevertheless, being rigidly and overtly suspicious of everyone is not appropriate. Hide your suspiciousness behind a veneer of curiosity. Be inquisitive, and maintain a questioning attitude (Nirenberg 1963), but never allow your suspicions to show. Asking questions accusingly or suspiciously may offend the interviewee or arouse fear or defensiveness, all of which will negatively affect cooperation. Questions full of genuine curiosity rather than accusatory suspicion will further your investigation.

There may come a time in the interview when it is appropriate to begin to reveal your suspicions. As you approach an interrogation, you might indicate that you sense the interviewee is not revealing important information. Through observation of an interviewee's verbal and nonverbal signals, the astute interviewer will evaluate whether or not the signals tend to indicate deceptive efforts. If an interviewer senses that an interviewee is being deceptive, the investigator may choose to enter into an interrogation or take some other logical path, such as the use of a polygraph examination.

IMAGINATION

Imagination has a part to play in the training of interviewers as well as in preparing for and conducting actual interviews. An excellent method for developing practical interviewing skills is to pool your ideas with one or more other imaginative interviewers. Group role playing can be used to test the ideas you generate. This approach allows the less imaginative and less assertive interviewers to benefit from their more skilled peers. Overly aggressive interviewers who think highly of their skills with people may learn, to their dismay, that there are interviewees who are more intelligent and more imaginative than they are (Nierenberg 1968). As general preparation for interviewing, strive to broaden your knowledge and awareness of other people in order to improve your ability to imagine the unimaginable.

Part of a successful interviewing venture is to try to consider why *you* might have done the crime. You should ask yourself questions like, What excuses might I have to steal, or molest, or murder, or sell secrets? Imagine the motivation of the thief or murderer while conducting the interview. Don't be surprised by any basis for the event under investigation—people justify, blame, and rationalize in ways that lack logic.

During an actual interview, use your imagination to anticipate possible contingencies and to plan the most effective responses. Your vicarious sensing through imagined participation allows you to better conceive the matter under investigation. An unimaginative investigator may think, "I could never imagine how a father could ever do such a thing to his daughter," while working on a molestation case. However, the most productive investigators have the ability to imagine the worst of human's inhumanity toward other people. Imagination is a special quality not shared by all investigators. Those who possess it naturally are fortunate for it is questionable whether imagination can be taught.

INTUITION

"The heart has reasons of which reason has no knowledge."

—*Pascal*

Imagination, knowledge, and awareness combine to produce intuition. Intuition has many other names: instinct, perception, gut feeling, hunch, sixth sense, third ear, reading between the lines, quick insight. It is the power of knowing through the senses, without recourse to inference or reasoning. As Edward Sapir (1884–1939), an American anthropologist who laid the foundation for modern linguistics, wrote: "We respond to gestures with an extreme alertness and, one might say, in accordance with an elaborate code that is written nowhere, known by none, and understood by all" (Sapir 1949, pp. 533–543). Most people possess a remarkable sensitivity to others, but their intuition remains dormant in the subconscious because it is never brought into play. The seeds of intuition are probably within you to be discovered, nurtured, and enhanced.

Although some people disregard intuition and consider its use unscholarly, I consider it to be a valuable asset in interviewing. Keen intuition is spontaneous, accurate, and helpful, but difficult to explain. In an interview, allow your intuitive judgment to help you select the investigative pathways you will pursue. Let your intuition direct the interview and guide your responses. In all of your interactions with interviewees, be alert to hints of facts and feelings revealed by a slip of the tongue, but conceal your interest. Subtle behavioral cues, words, gestures, and body language can direct you if you listen to your intuition. This is not to imply that you shouldn't plan your approach. Rather, a good balance is required. Acquiring a mental storehouse of information about human behavior is a must. As Alexander Pope so aptly said, "The proper study of mankind is man." With that study comes greater success.

Try to achieve a careful balance of the scientific and the intuitive so that you can avoid rigid procedures in your interviews.

Listen to your intuition during an interview, and allow it to guide you through sensitive issues. Otherwise, you will be unprepared for the spontaneous developments that occur in most interviews. As the Greek philosopher Heracleitus proclaimed around 500 B.C., "If you expect not the unexpected, ye shall not find the truth." Since seeking truth is your primary objective, you must expect the unexpected.

Trust yourself to understand what your intuition senses. Seemingly insignificant messages may help you develop the information you need. Bodily tension, flushing, excitability, frustration, evasiveness, and dejection can either confirm or contradict the interviewee's words. Actively listen by drawing on your knowledge and the storehouse of experiences in your subconscious. The subtleties of the interviewee's behavior can influence your judgment. Therefore, concentrate on using your intuition, knowledge, and experience to capture every subtlety you sense.

At first, you may not understand the apparently arbitrary techniques used by skilled interviewers. They frequently cannot explain the role of intuition in their interviewing process. Still, proficient interviewers confidently nurture their intuitive judgments and act on them. They sense the interviewee's tenseness and spontaneously select the words or actions that will encourage truthful responses. If you want to follow their example, you will have to learn how to trust your intuition. You will find that your total sensing of the situation, along with your common sense, is more trustworthy than your intellect.

In most worthwhile endeavors, the degree of your success is directly related to the effort you make. This applies equally to using intuition. Your hunches cannot bear fruit until you put them into action. Initially, rely on your self-confidence to implement your intuitive judgments, and be prepared to learn from your success or failure. Work through the various steps of interviewing, following the generally accepted concepts, but also work on developing techniques that capitalize on your intuitive talents. Use your intuition positively to read the interviewee's psychological movements, feelings, private logic or rationale, and any other signs that will help you achieve your goal.

The Intuition of Interviewees

Interviewees, too, are intuitive, and it would be foolhardy to ignore their ability to sense your judgments. In fact, through their exercise of their intuition, perhaps to achieve less-than-positive ends, they may have become quite skillful. Keenly alert to your signals, they respond positively or negatively to what they sense about you and your presentation. They scrutinize your every move and gesture, the delivery of your questions, and your reactions to their answers. Therefore, ask yourself these questions:

- Do I plan each interview in advance?
- Do I convey a calm composure?
- Do I spend whatever time is needed to complete the interview?
- Do I demonstrate that I care about the interviewee and am not just performing a routine job?
- Do I understand that displaying an accepting attitude toward all interviewees does not mean that I condone antisocial behavior and does not compromise my personal values?
- Do I understand that interviewees are secretly searching for a signal from me that it is indeed okay to be open and to reveal themselves?
- Do I consciously provide positive signals so that interviewees can count on my acceptance and fairness?
- Do I understand that I may subconsciously project dislike and censure during interviews, triggering hostile feelings, threatening rapport, and setting the stage for the interviewee to terminate the interview?

REVIEW QUESTIONS

1. How does your attitude influence the outcome of an interview?

2. Identify and discuss the three main components of a positive attitude.

3. What is the first step in changing your attitude?

4. In what ways does flexibility help during an interview?

5. Why strive to appear curious rather than suspicious?

6. What is the role of imagination in an interview?

7. What is intuition?

8. How can intuition be valuable to the interview process?

Evidence

All clues, all traces of evidence are valuable when solving a crime. Even small bits of evidence may help prove someone's guilt, while limiting the search for evidence may lead to charging the wrong person with the crime. Therefore, the search for guilt or innocence arises out of the examination of all available evidence.

REAL, DOCUMENTARY, AND TESTIMONIAL EVIDENCE

There are three basic types of evidence. Real and documentary evidence make up about 20 percent of all evidence presented in courts of law; testimonial evidence accounts for the remaining 80 percent.

Real, or physical, evidence is something you can photograph, chart, put your hands on, pick up, or store. It consists of tangible items, such as a bullet, a tire track, and a fingerprint. Real evidence is usually found at a crime scene and pertains to how the crime was committed and who is culpable. It is not based on the memory of the interviewee, unless it is found because a witness recalled where the shooter threw the gun or where the robber touched the bank counter. Such evidence is often volatile, fragile, and fleeting. It requires expert handling if it is to be useful in court. In handling real evidence, the investigator must maintain a chain of custody, which records how the evidence was handled, to prove that it was not contaminated in any way. Documentary evidence, on the other hand, is usually not found at a crime scene. Especially with crimes of passion, such as murder and assault, it is collected after the crime scene investigation has been completed. Documentary evidence often consists of a record or an account that will help investigators prove or disprove some fact. It includes such things as credit card receipts, hotel registers, and business records. Like real evidence, documentary evidence has substance. One difference is that real evidence is created as a by-product of a crime, while documentary evidence is often mandated or regulated in some way, such as records maintained in the normal course of business.

In many criminal investigations, such as cases of fraud or embezzlement, documents are the main form of evidence. Investigators of such white-collar crimes make a special effort to legally and quickly collect documents to preserve them as evidence. Often, search warrants or subpoenas are required to obtain stored business documents.

The part played by documentary evidence in an investigation is based on what the document contains. For example, data entered into a diary by a victim, a witness, or a suspect could be vital corroboration of other evidence discovered in other ways through such data contained in telephone records, receipts, and so forth. Motel records might verify that a person was a guest at the motel on a particular day. Other documents might confirm that a person was at a certain place at a particular time or was engaged in a specified activity.

Testimonial evidence generally comes from interviews of victims, witnesses, and suspects. It is given verbally but might subsequently be recorded in written form. Admissions and confessions gained through the interrogation of a subject are one kind of testimonial evidence.

Interviewing is the primary method of collecting testimonial evidence. Interviews are different from interrogations in that their objectives differ. The goal of interviewing is to collect truthful data to be used for informed decision making and just action taking. An interrogation, on the other hand, is a face-to-face meeting with a subject with the distinct objective of gaining an admission or a confession in a real or apparent violation of law or policy.

VOLUNTARY CONFESSIONS

A confession must be voluntary, or it will be rejected as evidence at a trial or administrative hearing. Seeking a confession from the interviewee is inappropriate, at least initially. However, if you seek to uncover the truth while treating the culpable interviewee with compassion, a confession may follow. To ensure that a confession holds up in court, follow proper procedures in arranging for the interrogation of the subject, as well as during the interrogation itself. A confession obtained after a "pickup" without probable cause (that is, reasonable grounds) to make an actual arrest may not be used as evidence (*Dunaway v. New York* [1979]).

Law enforcement officers must make it clear when a suspect is not under arrest and must document that the suspect is free to leave if he or she so desires. If the inquiry is held in an official location, such as a station house, it is imperative that interviewees comprehend that they are not being detained or in custody, if such is the case. Voluntary response is vital in these matters. To fight the admissibility of a confession in court, defense attorneys sometimes argue that psychological coercion was used to obtain the confession.

The *Miranda* Warnings

Before a person in police custody or otherwise deprived of freedom "in any significant way" may be interrogated, the following warnings must be given (*Miranda v. Arizona* [1966]):

1. You have a right to remain silent, and you need not answer any questions.
2. If you do answer questions, your answers can be used as evidence against you.
3. You have a right to consult with a lawyer before or during the questioning by the police.
4. If you cannot afford to hire a lawyer, one will be provided for you without cost.

These warnings have come to be known as the *Miranda* warnings, after the U.S. Supreme Court case in which they were enumerated.

The *Miranda* warnings apply only to "investigative custodial questioning aimed at eliciting evidence of a crime." Subjects in custody must understand what they are being told. The investigator is not permitted to bully them into talking once they decide not to do so, nor may the investigator attempt to dissuade them from speaking with a lawyer. This ensures that subjects in custody know that they have the right to remain silent (*Harryman v. Estelle* [1980]).

After receiving the required warnings and expressing willingness to answer questions, a subject in custody may legally be interrogated. It is unnecessary to embellish the *Miranda* warnings or to add new warnings. Similarly, it is unnecessary to use the exact language contained in *Miranda*. "Quite the contrary," said the Supreme Court. "*Miranda* itself indicated no talismanic incantation was required to satisfy its strictures."

When presenting the warnings, use advisement, not admonishment (*California v. Prysock* [1981]). In other words, state the four warnings without embellishing them. Merely expressing the warnings is sufficient; to do more is self-defeating. Some investigators earnestly urge the subject to grant permission for the interrogation; other investigators, directly or indirectly, strongly advise the subject not to grant permission. As you give the warnings, use a neutral tone and a matter-of-fact manner. This is not a time to caution, suggest, frighten, or admonish the person in custody.

When the *Miranda* Warnings Are Required

In 1976, the Supreme Court removed the misconception that the warnings must be given to anyone upon whom suspicion is "focused" (*Beckwith v. United States* [1976]; Inbau et al. 1986). Rather, the Court said, the warnings are required only when the subject is in police custody.

In an earlier case, the Court had defined "in police *custody* or otherwise deprived of freedom in any significant way" (the wording used in *Miranda v. Arizona* [1966]). The Court said that the key elements are "the time of the interrogation, the number of officers involved, and the apparent formal arrest of the subject" (*Orozco v. Texas* [1969]).

Regarding noncustodial interviewing within a police facility, the Supreme Court held that a noncustodial situation does not require the *Miranda* warnings simply because a reviewing court concludes that, even in the absence of any formal arrest or restraint of freedom of movement, the questioning took place in a "coercive environment" (*Oregon v. Mathiason* [1977]). The Court considered the circumstances of the interrogation when it provided this opinion:

> Any interview of one suspected of a crime by a police officer will have coercive aspects to it, simply by virtue of the fact that the police officer is part of a law enforcement system which may ultimately cause the suspect to be charged with a crime. But police officers are not required to administer *Miranda* warnings to everyone whom they question. Nor is the requirement of warnings to be imposed simply because the questioning takes place in the station house, or because the questioned person is one whom the police suspect. *Miranda* warnings are required only where there has been such a restriction on a person's freedom as to render him "in custody." It was that sort of coercive environment to which *Miranda* by its terms was made applicable, and to which it is limited.

Legally, *interrogation* is defined as asking a question, making a comment, displaying an object, or presenting a police report if this action calls for a response that may be incriminating. The subtle use of these actions make them "functional equivalents" of direct questions asked during an interrogation (*Brewer v. Williams* [1977]). This means that they, too, are bound by *Miranda,* but an exception can be found in *Rhode Island v. Innes* (1980).

If suspects who are not in custody freely consent to be interviewed or interrogated, there is no requirement that they be given the *Miranda* warnings. If an interviewee begins to confess without being interrogated, let him or her continue without interruption. When the confession has concluded, give the *Miranda* warnings to prevent any court from holding that custody began at the conclusion of the confession.

Subjects in custody can waive their constitutional rights. This is usually done in writing and signed, but oral waivers will suffice.

Police officers working private or part-time positions are bound by the *Miranda* ruling. If you are not conducting the investigation as a police officer, the *Miranda* decision does not affect you unless you are acting in cooperation with the police as a police agent. It's important to realize, however, that regardless of your role as an investigator, if you compel someone to confess, you are coercing a confession that will not hold up as legal evidence. Even though private security investigators generally do not have to administer the *Miranda* warnings, they still should not abuse subjects (*City of Grand Rapids v. Impens* [1982]).

LEGAL TACTICS WHEN SEEKING A CONFESSION

Be fair and practical when interrogating everyone, particularly suspects in custody. It is vital to avoid saying or doing anything that might cause an innocent person to confess. Do not use coercion, intimidation, threats, promises, or duress to force a confession; such action is neither legal nor acceptable. Intimidation reaps resentment, not truthful cooperation. Such tactics are self-defeating and inappropriate. The following legal tactics can be used during an interrogation:

- Exhibit confidence in the subject's culpability.
- Present circumstantial evidence to persuade the subject to tell the truth.
- Observe the subject's behavior for indications of deception.
- Empathize with and help the subject rationalize his or her actions and save face.
- Minimize the significance of the matter under investigation.
- Offer nonjudgmental acceptance of the subject's behavior.
- Point out the futility of not telling the truth.

Trickery and deceit are often used in interrogations. The U.S. Supreme Court gave tacit recognition to the necessity of these tactics in *Frazier v. Cupp* (1969). The Court held: "The fact that the police misrepresented the statements that [a suspected accomplice] had made is, while relevant, insufficient in our view to make this otherwise voluntary confession inadmissible. These cases must be decided by viewing the `totality of the circumstances.'"

EVIDENCE COLLECTION AND PRESERVATION

Strict rules govern the handling of all evidence before it is presented in court. The court that ultimately hears the evidence will want to know whether it was obtained legally, who handled it before it reached the court, and how. Does the evidence bear directly on the case, and does it accurately represent what happened? Was it tampered with in any way? Is it tainted? Before you begin to hunt for evidence, you must know what you're searching for, and that, in turn, depends on the objective of your investigation. If your objective is to prove intent in some criminal, civil, or administrative investigation, you may be looking for documents bearing a certain date or signature. If it is a hit-and-run case, the evidence may be skid marks or broken car parts. When interviewing an eyewitness, you may be searching for what the person heard or saw at the crime scene.

There is a difference, of course, between knowing what type of evidence you are looking for and searching only for evidence that suits some preconceived notion of who is culpable. Although having a theory or being guided by probabilities is generally acceptable, twisting the evidence to distort the truth is not. Professional investigators strive to maintain a neutral manner and an open mind so that they can impartially collect all available evidence.

If you obtain an admission or a confession, you will be challenged about how you obtained it. Did you determine that the interviewee was lying based on your intuition and observations?

As you collect evidence, be sure to make every effort to ensure that all evidence is obtained legally. Courts consider who was present, what was said, and how it was said when deciding whether to admit testimonial evidence. If evidence is contaminated by coercive tactics, threats, or illegal promises, we can expect a court to throw it out.

Even though you may collect massive amounts of evidence, not all of it will be pertinent to your investigation. You may interview fifty people and find only two who have useful information. Details of the other forty-eight interviews should not play a significant role in your report other than a notation that the interviews took place.

All evidence—real, documentary, and testimonial—can become contaminated. Preserving evidence and protecting it from contamination are vital to its successful presentation in court.

REPORT WRITING

Often, reports are official documents that detail how evidence was collected and preserved during an investigation. Hence, they are an important part of the chain of custody.

The technique of report writing can be learned by anyone who possesses two basic qualities: fundamental communication skills and a trained ability to observe. To be a competent investigator, you must write reports clearly so that everyone who reads them will know what you did and why.

Clear expression is not difficult to achieve, but it does take practice. When taking notes and writing your report, stick to the facts. A statement is the literal reproduction of the actual words spoken by the interviewee. Be a creative listener, use skillful phrases, and ask questions politely. First listen, then write notes. Be supportive and encouraging.

There are five basic steps in writing a report (Hess and Wrobleski 1988):

- Gather the facts (investigate, interview, interrogate).
- Record the facts immediately (take notes).
- Organize the facts.
- Write the report.
- Evaluate the report (edit and proofread; revise if necessary).

Good notes are a prerequisite for a good report, and they share many of the characteristics of a good report. When taking notes, organize your information; then report it in chronologically arranged paragraphs. Keep your writing straightforward and simple.

Characteristics of a Well-Written Report

A well-written report shows that you have done your job and that you recognize your responsibilities to the community you serve. A well-written report reflects positively on your education, your competence, and your professionalism, and it communicates better than a shoddily prepared report. Well-written reports share ten characteristics (Hess and Wrobleski 1988).

A well-written report is

- *Factual.* Facts make up the backbone of all reports. A fact is a statement that can be verified and known as a certainty. *Black's Law Dictionary* defines a *fact* as a thing done; an action performed or an incident transpiring; an event or circumstance; an actual occurrence. Present your facts, draw your conclusion, and stipulate which is which. A well-written report does not contain unidentified opinions.

- *Accurate.* Just as there are rules for spelling, capitalization, and punctuation, there are rules for word choice. Ensure accuracy by being specific in your language and by choosing the most appropriate words for each situation. Avoid jargon, which creates confusion.
- *Objective.* A good report is fair and impartial. Subjective writing might be more colorful than objective writing, but it has no place in a report. You can ensure objectivity in your reports by including all relevant facts and by avoiding words with emotional overtones. Specific types of crime require different information, but you will frequently need certain general information. The *who, what, when,* and *where* questions should be answered by factual statements. The *how* and *why* statements may require inferences on your part. When this is the case, and especially when addressing the question of motive, clearly label your opinions.
- *Complete.* A report should give as full an account as possible. To avoid slanting your report, record all possible motives reported to you, no matter how implausible they may seem.
- *Concise.* The information you choose to include should be worded as concisely as possible; no one wants to read a wordy report. You can reduce wordiness two ways: (1) Leave out unnecessary information, and (2) use as few words as possible to record the necessary facts.
- *Clear.* Clarity, one of the most important characteristics of a well-written report, is discussed in detail below.
- *Mechanically correct.* Be sure to use correct spelling, capitalization, and punctuation in your report. A report riddled with these types of errors gives a poor impression of its writer and the writer's actions.

- *Written in standard English.* When you translate your ideas into words, follow the rules for correct writing. Use the past tense, complete sentences, and good grammar.
- *Legible.* An illegible report gives a poor impression of the writer and a distorted explanation of who said what.
- *On time.* A report that is submitted late reflects negatively on the report writer.

Make your reports, like all of your other communications, as clear and direct as possible. The following suggestions will help ensure that your reports can be easily understood (Hess and Wrobleski 1988):

- Use the first person. That is, write "I" instead of "the investigator" or "the interviewer." First-person writing is recommended for law enforcement reports because it is direct.
- Write in the active voice. For example, say, "I asked Jane Smith . . ." rather than "Jane Smith was asked . . ." The active voice clearly indicates who performed the action.
- Correctly modify details to be included.
- When using pronouns, be sure it is clear to whom they refer.
- Use parallelism. That is, use the same type of structure for similar parts of a sentence.
- Choose your words carefully. Avoid legal, technical, unfamiliar, and slang words.
- Include specific, concrete facts and details.
- Keep descriptive words and phrases as close as possible to the words they describe.
- Use diagrams and sketches to clarify a complex description.

TESTIMONY IN A COURT OF LAW

Testimonial evidence is the foundation of both criminal and civil litigation and is often the subject of cross-examination.

Evidence presented for consideration in court cannot intentionally be tainted. It cannot be tampered with and still be credible and trustworthy.

True professionals maintain the integrity of the evidence and deserve society's honor and respect.

During a trial, attorneys often seek to impeach, or discredit, witnesses for the opposing side. Most states allow the credibility of a witness to be attacked during a trial. This is usually done by challenging the truthfulness and consistency of the witness's statements. Investigators are obligated to tell the truth whether in court or when giving a legal deposition. "From the opposing attorney's point of view, the purpose of the deposition is to create a record for future impeachment. The deposition process can be a lengthy one. Be patient. . . . Hide your desire to get it over with. Show toughness and resolve and a willingness to stay as long as necessary" (Matson, Jack V., pp. 41–42).

REVIEW QUESTIONS

1. Identify the three types of evidence, and give two examples of each.

2. What is the difference between interviewing and interrogating?

3. Why must a confession be voluntary, and what might happen if a confession is not obtained voluntarily?

4. What are the four *Miranda* warnings?

5. When are you legally required to give the *Miranda* warnings? Discuss specific situations.

6. How has the U.S. Supreme Court defined *interrogation?*

7. Is a confession legal if a private security person compels someone to confess?

8. Identify at least three legal interrogation tactics.

9. Is it permissible to use trickery when trying to obtain a confession?

10. Why is it important for the court to consider "the totality of the circumstances" under which evidence is located, collected, and preserved?

11. List the five basic steps in writing a report.

12. What are the ten characteristics of a well-written report?

13. What is a fact?

14. How can you ensure objectivity in your reports?

15. What can you do to make your reports clear?

5

Public and Private Interviewing

Whether from the public or private sector, first-class investigators resemble each other more than they differ. They are successful because they share well-practiced skills, a high degree of perception, and a positive attitude. For the purposes of this chapter, we will define *public investigators* as official law enforcement agents, such as state or local police officers. We will define *private investigators* as licensed private detectives and the security or loss prevention personnel of a company. While the number of investigators in the public sector generally remains steady, the number of investigators in the private sector is growing. This chapter reviews some distinctions between the kinds of crimes public and private detectives investigate (with particular attention to white-collar crime) and the procedures they use.

Before we continue, let's take a brief look at how crime is reported and classified in the United States. City, county, and state law enforcement agencies keep track of the yearly incidence of different crimes in their jurisdictions. Compiled by volume and frequency, these statistics are sent to the Federal Bureau of Investigation (FBI), which issues the annual *Uniform Crime Report*. The FBI classifies the most serious crimes, such as murder, rape, and robbery, as "Part I offenses." These crimes, which are the most likely to be reported to the police, serve as the major index of crime in the United States. The crimes listed as "Part II offenses" are considered less serious—that is, less harmful to individuals and less damaging to society. The Part I and Part II offenses are listed in the following box. As you can see, the FBI considers fraud and embezzlement to be Part II offenses. The federal guidelines define *fraud* as "fraudulent conversion and obtaining money or property by false pretenses (confidence games and bad checks, except forgeries and counterfeiting, are included)" and *embezzlement* as "the misappropriation or misapplication of money or property entrusted to one's care, custody, or control" (FBI 2001, p. 407).

PART I AND PART II OFFENSES OF THE *UNIFORM CRIME REPORT*

Part I Offenses	*Part II Offenses*
Murder	Other assaults
Rape	Forgery and counterfeiting
Robbery	Fraud
Aggravated assault	Embezzlement
Burglary	Stolen property offenses
Larceny	Vandalism
Motor vehicle theft	Weapons offenses
Arson	Prostitution
	Other sex offenses
	Drug-law violations

Part II Offenses (continued)

Gambling

Family-related offenses (e.g., abuse and neglect)

Driving under the influence (DUI)

Liquor-law violations

Disorderly conduct

Other offenses

Fraud and embezzlement cost American businesses billions of dollars each year. To control their losses, many companies have established their own security or loss prevention staffs to investigate these crimes. More often than not, the police are never notified when these crimes occur.

INVESTIGATIONS IN THE PUBLIC AND PRIVATE SPHERES

Traditionally, private investigators have dealt with fraud and embezzlement, while the police have handled the violent crimes of murder, rape, and assault. Until just recently, law enforcement officers were not properly trained to investigate sophisticated white-collar crimes. Rather, police training was reactive in nature, emphasizing how to diffuse violent situations, how to perform first aid, how to shoot straight, and such topics. The subtle aspects of human interaction, the gentle art of communication, and their usefulness in investigative interviewing were all but ignored.

Today, businesses call upon private investigators to look into various offenses committed against the company or its employees. Many large businesses have trained detectives on staff to investigate crimes ranging from stalking to theft. Typically, if a Part I offense has occurred, the internal investigation is turned over to the appropriate police agency. However, if the incident can be investigated by internal security personnel, it is. Few companies want the embarrassment of a public disclosure of their problems. In addition, many businesses do not think law enforcement agencies can properly investigate so-called white-collar crimes.

In the private sector, private detectives and security personnel for corporations might investigate something even though no civil or criminal matter is pending. The investigation might be aimed specifically at providing information to help management make administrative decisions regarding the violation of company rules or procedures. Often, the evidence collected never reaches the outside world or the civil or criminal courts. The decision to reveal or not reveal the evidence to the public depends on what's ultimately best for the company.

Police agencies investigate few embezzlement cases. The vast majority of such cases are handled by private investigators. Why aren't police agencies involved in the investigation of more white-collar crimes?

Based upon my forty years' experience, I am convinced that businesses, and banks in particular, do not want their internal matters revealed to the public. Reports of internal theft lead to bad press. That is, if internal losses become public knowledge, the bank's image as a safe place to deposit money will suffer.

At one time, the FBI investigated all internal and other bank thefts, and technically it still retains jurisdiction. But today, the bureau does not investigate cases involving losses of only a few thousand dollars. The bureau has shifted its priorities, leaving local police agencies to investigate most cases of fraud and embezzlement. Unfortunately, local police agencies are generally not properly trained in these investigations, and even if they were, most bank managers would still prefer to handle the matter privately.

THE COLLECTION OF EVIDENCE

Whether the investigator is a police detective, the loss prevention officer of a large corporation, or a private investigator hired to look into a particular incident, he or she must operate within predefined parameters when conducting an investigation and collecting evidence. Police investigators must work within federal and state laws intended to protect society from unreasonable police behavior. In addition, they work within the bureaucracy and operating procedures of their respective agencies. Private investigators have a wider choice of investigative methods because there are fewer laws governing their actions. A company's internal investigators may take investigative liberties that might seem unreasonable, but their actions do not affect society generally. Still, their behavior is limited and controlled by company policy, and the fear of possible civil suits. Company control of an investigator's behavior, generally, cannot influence the inquiry to such an extent to cause the investigator to violate personal ethics and professional responsibilities. If this happens, there is a question of integrity.

Regardless of whether an offense is investigated by public or private detectives, the evidence needed to prosecute the case is the same. If a piece of evidence is to be of value to a company (or, for that matter, to society), the methods used to collect and preserve it must meet the highest standards imposed by the courts. This is true even when the evidence collected serves only to justify an employee's dismissal rather than prosecution in court. The case may turn ugly if the fired employee sues the company for wrongful termination and the company must produce the evidence on which it based the termination. If evidence collection and preservation fall short of acceptable standards, the company may be in deep trouble financially. In the public sector, of course, if a police investigator does not collect and preserve evidence properly, the prosecution may dissolve, allowing the guilty party to go free.

TESTIMONIAL EVIDENCE

Obviously, the main topic of this book is the collection of testimonial evidence through investigative interviewing. Most, if not all, of the offenses cataloged in the FBI's *Uniform Crime Report* require investigative interviewing of victims, witnesses, and suspects. Most of the evidence presented during the prosecution of Part I and Part II offenses was obtained in an interview or interrogation.

There are legal means available to assist both public and private investigators in searching out all forms of evidence that will reveal the truth. Subpoenas, for example, help investigators collect evidence without resorting to illegal methods.

As this book points out, the investigator's major job is to persuade the interviewee to cooperate long enough to reveal truthful information about the crime under investigation. To this end, investigators of all kinds must cultivate professional attitudes and techniques that promote communication and cooperation. While most interviewees will acquiesce to requests for information, they need encouragement from the investigator. There is always some resistance to an investigator's inquiries. Some people believe that the degree of resistance depends on the nature of the offense under investigation. I, however, believe that the degree of resistance is a reflection of the interviewee's personality, the interviewer's attitude, and the qualities the interviewer brings to bear on the interview.

Are people more likely to refuse to cooperate with a private investigation than with a police investigation? Certainly, people perceive less of a threat from private investigations. Most consider losing a job to be less damaging than being fined or going to jail. Employees are expected to cooperate in reasonable inquiries undertaken by company management. The refusal to cooperate in an investigation is often regarded by management as insubordination and sufficient cause for dismissal. But it does not prove that the employee is guilty.

Occasionally, the greater threat of a police investigation works to obscure, rather than reveal, the truth. Because of the fear that a police interview can inspire, interviewees feel pressured to provide answers that they sense the investigator wants—and thus lead the police to a wrongful arrest. During the 1980s, police officers in Minnesota investigated charges of child sexual molestation. Because of the interviewing tactics they used, some of the officers were sued. (They were later exonerated.) The court's opinion in that case (see box below) reveals how difficult it can be for police investigators to discover the truth while simultaneously protecting the rights of the alleged victims and the accused. It also highlights the need for comprehensive training in interviewing at the beginning, and throughout, a police officer's career. As this case demonstrates, damage suits are possible even when officers believe they are doing their job properly. Legal norms for interviewing tactics are based upon respect for the rights of the interviewee, no matter what his or her age.

REPORT ON SCOTT COUNTY INVESTIGATIONS BY MINNESOTA ATTORNEY GENERAL HUBERT H. HUMPHREY III

In working with child sex abuse it is not unusual for children to initially deny being abused. In subsequent interviews they may finally admit what happened. However, the Scott County cases raise the issue of how long and how often one can continue to question children about abuse before running the risk of false accusation.

While the record contains examples of investigative mistakes and flawed interrogation, particularly from the standpoint of successful prosecution of those implicated by children who have experienced extensive questioning, an imperfect investigation without more evidence does not deprive the investigators of qualified immunity. Immunity is forfeited for the questioning function upon at least a preliminary showing that the interrogation so exceeded clearly established legal norms for this function that reasonable persons in the detectives' position would have known their conduct was illegal. . . .

We conclude that the interviewing conduct occurred in a gray area of investigative procedure as to which there were, and probably still are, less than clearly established legal norms. The gray area referred to involves the extent to which juvenile suspected victims may reasonably be questioned, particularly if they initially deny abuse, and the extent to which leading questions, confrontation with reports by others, and photographs of suspects may be used. . . .

We do not consider the standards for the interrogation of juvenile witnesses and victims, particularly in the area of sexual abuse, so clearly established in 1984 that on the basis of hindsight the deputies should now be forced to defend their questioning techniques in these damage suits.

REVIEW QUESTIONS

1. How are public and private investigators alike? What is their biggest challenge?

2. What is the difference between Part I and Part II offenses? Give three examples of each.

3. How does the FBI define *fraud* and *embezzlement?*

4. Is white-collar crime a significant problem in the United States? Explain.

5. What types of crimes do public investigators usually handle? What about private investigators?

6. Are police officers properly trained in the investigation of white-collar crimes? Explain.

7. Why aren't the police asked to investigate more cases of fraud, embezzlement, and internal theft?

8. Compare the responsibilities of public and private investigators when collecting and preserving evidence, and describe the consequences for each of failing to follow proper procedures.

9. How do public and private investigations differ when it comes to interviewing?

10. Why is it usually necessary for the investigator to encourage interviewees to be cooperative?

11. Are people more likely to comply with a public investigation or a private one?

12. How might false accusations become a problem when interviewing children in sex-abuse cases?

6

Rapport and Active Listening

Interviews are not normal social encounters in which two people exchange ideas and experiences on an equal footing. In an investigative interview, the interviewee should do most of the talking while the investigator acts as a catalyst, a persuader, and a stimulator of thoughts. The catalyst promotes an unspoken chemistry that produces cooperation. He or she asks appropriate questions to probe for facts, anecdotes, and feelings from the interviewee (Sherwood 1972). To prepare for your role as interviewer-catalyst, look at each inquiry with clear thinking as you plan your approach. Detach yourself from the emotional content of the interview, adopt a positive attitude, and be flexible. In your role as catalyst, two basic interviewing tactics will prove useful: building rapport and active listening. We will look at each technique in turn.

BUILDING RAPPORT

Mutual confidence and trust are difficult to establish in an interview, and the interviewee is not always your partner in seeking the truth. While your goal is to determine the truth in an investigation, the interviewee's goal might be to protect himself from a variety of harms (Woody and Woody 1972, p. 210). You can overcome this obstacle and encourage interviewees to provide information by building rapport. If you can plan, organize, and evoke cooperation in social situations, you probably possess basic qualities of leadership and can establish rapport, inspire confidence, elicit information, and keep interviews under control.

"Rapport is the good feeling or warmth that exists between people"; it is an "interpersonal relationship characterized by a spirit of cooperation, confidence and harmony" (Coleman 1976, p. 750). In an interview, rapport is like an electric current that flows between participants. It is based on how they communicate rather than on what they say, and it requires practiced effort. "Rapport involves building a degree of comfortableness together, of trust in one another, and of basic goodwill that will permit nondefensive interaction" (Downs et al. 1980, p. 57). To develop rapport is to create a feeling within yourself and the interviewee of alertness, well-being, and even excitement. Rapport is a psychological closeness established in the very beginning of an interview, when you blend your verbal and nonverbal actions with those of the interviewee (Nirenberg 1963). The first few minutes are crucial: "Research has shown that people form their basic impressions of one another during the first few minutes of an interview" (Quinn and Zunin 1972, pp. 8–14). Rapport is important in an interview because the degree of rapport you establish determines the degree of compliance you obtain from the interviewee.

Investigators who succeed in establishing rapport with interviewees demonstrate their empathy with them and generally obtain their truthful cooperation. They feel less inhibited in asking questions, even questions about sensitive or personal matters, and interviewees are less resistant about answering (Davis 1975). The development of rapport does not require that the interviewer become emotionally involved or that the interviewer's commitment, persistence, or objectivity be eroded. You are not trying to become the interviewee's best buddy. You are trying to solve the case. You want the interviewee to buy into your friendliness only long enough so that you can obtain the information you need. When all is said and done, no one will misunderstand your behavior.

Active listening, discussed later in this chapter, is an important technique for building rapport, but there are others. "You can build rapport through small talk, a good orientation, and a very warm, friendly manner" (Downs et al. 1980, p. 201). To achieve rapport with the interviewee, try to find an area of common interest: "Call attention to ways in which you and the other person are similar. . . . You can call attention to similarities in such subtle ways as by complimenting the person (thus showing that you have similar tastes) or by identifying a common gripe" (Downs et al. 1980, p. 259).

You can also build rapport by enhancing the interviewee's self-image. If your inquiry is handled in a professional way, so that cooperation will benefit the interviewee's self-image, he or she will feel honored to cooperate and will later be proud of assisting "the authorities" (Nierenberg 1968). Be sure to make your inquiry relevant to the interviewee's here-and-now life and concerns (Bennis et al. 1973, p. 199). Your attitude is communicated by the ways you listen and ask questions. People find it flattering to be asked for their opinions. In an interview, this compliments the interviewee's views, strengthens rapport, and shows your respect (Nirenberg 1963, p. 23). Expressions of genuine interest and empathy, positive recognition, easy eye contact, and appropriate positive silences also help build and maintain rapport.

At the beginning of an interaction, the interviewee may display signs of uneasiness. Even truthful interviewees may have some anxiety over whether you will be fair and unbiased in your methods (Nirenberg 1963). As rapport develops, you may notice a distinct sigh of relief, signaling a lessening of the interviewee's distress and the building of trust. From that point onward, the interview may take on a more relaxed character.

You need to be alert to whether the interviewee is truly listening. Just because interviewees are silent and appear to be listening does not mean that they are truly receptive to what you are saying. They may be lost in an emotional maze of fear. Periodically ask questions designed to test whether the interviewee is listening. A blank, unresponsive stare may signal distress, unclear thinking, or an imbalanced mental process.

Control your emotions without losing your enthusiasm. Keep your thoughts collected and composed; think your comments through carefully before presenting them to the interviewee. Refuse to become ruffled, and keep your goal clearly in mind. The use of sarcasm, ridicule, or cynicism creates tension that does not help to build rapport and gain the interviewee's cooperation (Benjamin 1974, p. 153). "Most people resist being thought of as inferior; therefore, they would be very reluctant to establish rapport with or to be persuaded by anyone who tries, consciously or unconsciously, to make them feel inferior" (Downs et al. 1980, p. 264). Instead, help the interviewer to rationalize and save face. Other actions that tend to block rapport are making negative comments, engaging in monologues, second-guessing the interviewee, displaying a condescending attitude, and trying to hurry through the interview (Downs et al. 1980, p. 201).

Through participant role reversal, an interviewee may skillfully unseat you and take over the role of leader in the interview. An inexperienced interviewer may not see the signals and may discover too late that he or she has given up command of the interview, answering rather than asking questions. This role reversal is embarrassing only if it continues. Proficient interviewers realize when role reversal is taking place and immediately regain control without making it too obvious or causing conflict. Entering into a power struggle with interviewees creates alienation instead of friendly rapport (Nirenberg 1963).

When ending an unsuccessful interview, do nothing to create hard feelings. Even when hostile interviewees refuse to answer your questions, don't hold a grudge, show no disgust, frustration, or anger, and don't allow yourself to vent your displeasure. Don't allow your pride to cause you to blame interviewees for their lack of cooperation. Instead, lay a positive foundation for future interviews. Aim to have all interviewees leave with a positive feeling, allowing them to believe that they experienced a meaningful and valuable interaction.

ACTIVE LISTENING

> "His thoughts were slow, his words were few, and never made to glisten. But he was a joy wherever he went. You should have heard him listen."
>
> —*Anonymous*

There are two main conditions of listening: the passive (inattentive) and the active (attentive). Most of us are good at passive listening. We appear to be listening when, in fact, our minds have wandered off. Too often, our need to talk is greater than our ability to listen.

To become an effective interviewer, you should learn to overcome this human failing (Benjamin 1974, p. 86). A good interviewer is a good listener (Dexter 1970, p. 111). By staying keenly aware of the important role of active listening in an interview, you can analyze and encourage in a meaningful way. You can use active listening skills to determine the interviewee's frame of reference and to reduce emotional tension. Rely on your spontaneity, sensitivity, and basic common sense; listen better and understand more. Avoid putting on a show of authority, displaying more interest in yourself and your role than in listening to the interviewee.

Most people feel that no one really listens to them. They appreciate an opportunity to show their knowledge and to express their ideas and feelings (Bennis et al. 1973, p. 541). They hunger for that feeling of importance when approached for their views.

The first step in empathizing is to listen and attempt to grasp the meaning of what is said. Your effort to listen actively demonstrates your recognition of the interviewee's worth and encourages continued cooperation. Active listening involves your total person and must be a part of your presentation. You can exhibit your attentiveness to the interviewee through the intonation of your voice, the positioning of your body, and your facial expressions. By questioning, accepting, rephrasing, reflecting, and pausing, you can signal that you are listening (Nirenberg 1963).

The important tactic of active listening requires attentiveness and concentration, acceptance, detachment, and patience. We will discuss each of these qualities before exploring in more detail how the interviewer can signal active listening.

Attentiveness and Concentration

> "Finding the perfect listener, gaining that sense of relaxation from being able to talk or not talk when one wants to, is one of the greater pleasures."
>
> —*Eliot D. Chapple (Anthropologist, as quoted in Davis 1975, p. 117)*

With a little effort, you can learn to be a "perfect listener": Be alert and courteous, give the interviewee your undivided attention, and be ready with appropriate questions or comments to show interest in what the interviewee says. The benefits of such attentiveness are numerous. There is a close connection between active listening and intuition; active listening helps you sense meanings that are not revealed in words alone. The development of rapport is built upon a foundation partly made up of your ability to show that you are listening. Your attentiveness implies acceptance and encourages the interviewee to say more. It allows the interviewee to sense the genuine, unplanned, spontaneous you. In the end, being attentive to the interviewee helps you achieve your ultimate goal: gathering truthful information.

Give the interviewee your full attention. Ponder, at least momentarily, each of the interviewee's comments. People can sense if you are truly interested by the subtle way you pause to reflect on what they say. As an active listener, your attention should not be fickle or fragile or fall apart at the least distraction or promise of pleasure, excitement, or frustration (Nirenberg 1963).

Avoid an indifferent attitude. One way of turning people off is to not pay attention to their comments—to be thinking of the next question to ask and not devoting yourself fully to the emotion of the moment. Preoccupied glances, slack body posture, and inappropriate silences and comments all imply boredom. Inattentive listeners do not truly hear what is being said; they superficially signal hearing and responding, but no real thoughts are formulated. They are a bit out of rhythm with the conversation and the mood of the interaction. In a fast-moving interview, they fail to provide sharp, alert, quick responses.

People can sense when you are preoccupied, bored, or inattentive. Interviewees who sense that you are bored or that your interest is not genuine may feel used by you. When facing an inattentive listener, they tend to regard the interaction as a waste of time and may hold back information. Because they may not outwardly express their reasons for withdrawing, you may never realize that your inattention stopped the flow of information.

Active listening means concentrating on what is and what is not being said—both verbally and nonverbally (Nierenberg 1968). Evaluate the interviewee's subjective comments in light of his or her emotional state, attitudes, and values. Use every advantage to analyze the story you hear to make it sensible (Woody and Woody 1972, p. 147). Attempt to determine the interviewee's frame of reference, and be guided by what you learn (Dexter 1970, p. 19). Evaluating interviewees properly helps you determine how hurriedly you can conduct the interview and what direction it should take. Interviewees who feel rushed may sense that you are insincere in your efforts, and they may become less cooperative (Wicks 1972).

Always be alert for signals of the interviewee's mental processes, and look for clues of motivation and hidden needs. As you listen to what the interviewee has to say, continually observe the way he or she acts. Through mannerisms, gestures, recurrent phrases, and modes of expression, interviewees signal their thinking, their hidden needs, and possible deception. Avoid idle thinking by concentrating on the specifics of the interview. Get into the mood of data gathering, and listen constructively. Allowing the interviewee's comments to glide over the surface of your mind is self-defeating (Nirenberg 1963). Concentrate!

Some inexperienced interviewers are so busy thinking of their next question that they forget to listen to the interviewee's answers. Devious interviewees can take advantage of the investigator's inattention by making innocuous comments or failing to answer questions. If you don't concentrate your thinking, deceptive interviewees with moderate skills can too easily mislead you. Even evasive interviewees, who are not really deceptive but only reluctant or hesitant to comply, can mislead you if you aren't paying attention. Some interviewees play mental games with authority figures to test their sincerity (Nirenberg 1963).

Acceptance

The listener who exhibits nonjudgmental understanding, who provides empathic responses, encourages others to continue to communicate. By actively listening to interviewees, you signal your acceptance of them, and they intuitively sense that it is okay to talk to you. Empathize with their attitudes, the roles they are playing, their expressed and demonstrated needs.

Like most people, interviewees often think that what they have to say is the most important thing in the world, and they continually evaluate their listeners. If you are receptive, understanding, warm, responsive, interested, and involved, interviewees will probably enter a dialogue with you. They are responsive in a productive, permissive atmosphere. While interviewees expect and appreciate appropriate responses to their comments, they don't necessarily seek an evaluation. They need reassurance, support, and acceptance while revealing their thoughts and exposing their secrets. Recognizing the interviewee's dignity, worth, and importance, and helping the interviewee strive for self-expression, self-realization, and self-fulfillment, improves the productivity of the interview. Sensing your helping, friendly attitude, the interviewee will probably cooperate as expected.

The ideal interviewer listens with nonjudgmental understanding and does not criticize or admonish (Garrett 1972, p. 20). By exhibiting genuine interest, you can avoid injecting your opinions, value judgments, and criticisms into the interview. When interviewees sense that you are evaluating them with your personal set of values, they may become defensive, which will curtail the flow of information. Try to maintain a universal set of values as well as your personal set of values. Neatly tuck your personal values away when you interview. Maintain the attitude that no behavior is too aggressive, no feeling too guilty or shameful, for the interviewee to bring into the interview.

Use sounds and actions to signal your acceptance of the interviewee. Murmur vocal sounds like "uh-huh" at appropriate times during the interview. Display facial expressions and use gestures that demonstrate attentiveness (Davis 1975; Downs et al. 1980, p. 78). If the interviewee talks spontaneously, avoid interrupting until there is a significant pause. Encourage the interviewee to continue by nodding your head and paying careful attention to the interviewee's words (Woody and Woody 1972, p. 154).

Detachment

Occasionally you may need to investigate crimes that are so horrible that they shake you to your very core or turn your stomach. As you investigate crimes that would anger any normal citizen, you may feel distracted by intense internal dissonance, an absence of internal harmony (Bennis et al. 1973, p. 203). When you are expected to remain calm and listen, your body cannot vent the pent-up pressure caused by stress. No matter what the circumstances, don't be thrown off balance. Don't become so angry that you want to seek revenge on behalf of the victim. Remain detached, and gain the interviewee's cooperation by treating him or her with kindness, decency, and human dignity (Nierenberg 1968). Being somewhat depersonalized helps the interviewer react with calm acceptance toward the interviewee.

Be secure in your personal identity. Understand yourself, and maintain a sturdy philosophical core around your personal and cultural values. Learn to use self-selected identities without "injuring" the core of your personality (Dexter 1970, p. 27).

When interviewees respond to your questions in an angry outburst, detach yourself and be ready to withstand the heat. Don't react in a defensive, defiant manner. You might say, "I see your point of view," or "I understand what you mean." You will only alienate the interviewee if you react to emotional tirades with threats and insults or if you fall back on your position of authority and demand that the interviewee remain civil (Nierenberg 1968).

Patience

> "If thou art one to whom petition is made, be calm as thou listenest to what the petitioner has to say. Do not rebuff him before he has swept out his body or before he has said that for which he came. The petitioner likes attention to his words better than the fulfilling of that for which he came. . . . It is not necessary that everything about which he has petitioned should come to pass, but a good hearing is soothing to the heart."
>
> —*The instruction of PTAH–HOTEP, 3000 B.C., to his son (Gunn 1918)*

Inexperienced interviewers often rush from one question to another without waiting for an answer. They fail to understand that patience is a necessary component of active listening (Dexter 1970, p. 112). Impatience signals ridicule, cynicism, and intimidation and blocks rapport. Impatience toward interviewees is self-defeating and can only be characterized as abusive and judgmental. Rather than use rapid-fire questions, proficient interviewers allow interviewees time to answer fully without interruption, thereby showing interest and attentiveness. By speaking softly, slowly, and firmly, they signal that they are capable of both comprehending and solving the investigative problem. With composure, serenity, and emotional strength, they advance toward their goal. That calmness and strength are patience at work.

To be a good listener, you should take the backseat and allow the interviewee time to talk (Wicks and Josephs 1972). As they talk, interviewees generally begin to feel comfortable enough to reveal the information you need. Avoid making superfluous comments, and remain alert to what is going on moment by moment (Nirenberg 1963). It is through expressed emotion at times of tension that interviewees test your sincerity, compassion, and caring (Garrett 1972, p. 50). Your patience in an interview signals tolerance, acceptance, and understanding while it stimulates dialogue. Patience carries with it forgiveness and respect for interviewees. Painstakingly and patiently advance point by point and item by item toward your goal. If the interviewee becomes hostile or indignant, try to remain calm and appeal for cooperation. "Be patient and persistent to overcome hidden, irrational interviewee opposition" (Nirenberg 1963, p. 132). Do not rebuff the interviewee. As Benjamin Disraeli, the late British prime minister, said, "Next to knowing when to seize an advantage, the most important thing in life is to know when to forego an advantage."

Your patience is vital in the face of an emotional outburst. A sensitive response to a victim or witness in distress is essential in reducing the person's fear. Permit interviewees to discharge their stored anger or pain in an emotional dumping process. Listen to interviewees as though you think they have something worthwhile to offer. Your patience gives interviewees time to rid themselves of tension (Wicks and Josephs 1972). However, they may enter into a meandering conversation to rest and to test the degree of your patience (Nirenberg 1963). The strength of your gentleness, patience, and kindness leads to confidence in your judgment.

Be alert to both concrete and abstract information. Concrete, objective explanations paint a clear picture of the event or situation. Abstract, subjective comments are emotional, nonspecific, and often misleading. Strive to obtain concrete information, but accept that the interviewee will also express emotion and make many subjective comments. Take comfort and reassurance from William Keefe's comment that "eventually [the interviewer] may spend less time as he winnows more skillfully the valuable information from the valueless" (Keefe 1971, p. 24).

As your career progresses, you will come in contact with many different personality types. Some interviewees are impulsive, egotistical, and childish, with a low tolerance for frustration. Others are better at controlling their impulses and will seek to collaborate with you to solve the crime. Your patience can guide the inquiry, no matter what personality type you need to interview.

SIGNALING ACTIVE LISTENING

Although verbal communication is the most distinctive of human achievements, nonverbal communication, including body language, touch, and positive silence, is equally important. Feelings and intentions are conveyed through body posture and movement, gestures, facial expressions, and eye contact. In fact, expectations are conveyed mostly through nonverbal communication. Nonverbal communication, which is learned throughout life, reveals underlying personality traits, subconscious attitudes, intentions, and conflicts. Use it to your advantage in an interview. Express your willingness to listen to the interviewee by engaging your whole body in the communication process and not merely your words. Move forward in your chair, nod your head, wear a curious expression, and smile to encourage the interviewee to continue speaking. Some interviewers are highly skilled in the use of nonverbal communication. Others can learn how to use body language, touch, and positive silence to express their positive expectations and willingness to listen.

Body Language

Body language includes posture, movement, gestures, facial expression, and eye contact. It is an important part of the climate of an interview, which is in play from the beginning to the end of the encounter. You will convey your expectations to the interviewee through your body language. During an interview, your nonverbal behavior is under constant scrutiny, and a single negative message has the potential to render an entire interview ineffective. Before you utter your first word, the interviewee will examine you for signs of acceptance and trustworthiness. Your only defense is to display positive and believable signals of acceptance. A subtle delivery is needed to avoid the appearance of pretense and to avoid arousing the interviewee's suspicion. Use your tone of voice, deliberate silences, variations in eye contact, facial expressions, distancing, and posture to express positive or negative feelings (*Communication* 1975).

Body Posture and Movement

Signal that you are paying attention to the interviewee by sharing postures, by standing or sitting close, and by facing the interviewee squarely or at a 45-degree angle. Move slowly and confidently to avoid scaring the interviewee. Lean forward to show that you are warm and attentive. When you disagree with something the interviewee has said, be careful not to allow your posture or movement to announce your disagreement. People generally shift their position before voicing their disagreement with what the speaker has said (Scheflen 1964).

When you sense that you are communicating effectively with an interviewee, begin to move in synchrony with him or her, signaling attentive listening (Davis 1975). Try to move in time to the rhythm of the speaker. People are drawn to those who seem to mirror them. Just as a perfect meshing of gears is essential to a smooth-running engine, an effective meshing of personalities is key to a successful interview.

Gestures, Facial Expression, and Tone of Voice

Proficient investigators use nonconfrontational interviewing tactics, and their body language reflects their nonconfrontational style. If your gestures are in any way accusatory—for example, by pointing your finger—the interviewee will become defensive. When gesturing, display your total involvement in what is being said. Keep your arms open and your palms extended. Turn your head toward the interviewee; do not look at him or her out of the corner of your eye. Look at the interviewee often, and wear an interested or pleased expression. Your face will not crack and break if you flex your facial muscles to show expression! Be careful not to indicate an authoritarian attitude with your facial expressions or intonation, though. Phrases like "I see," "Please go on," and "Uh-huh" indicate interest and desire to hear more (Woody and Woody 1972, p. 165). But the impact of these phrases can be negative or positive depending on how they are expressed. You might say, "Please go on," but stop the flow of information with a tone that proclaims disbelief or boredom. Collect evidence in a fair and impartial manner by keeping your tone alert and neutral.

Eye Contact

The interviewer's easy eye contact promotes rapport with the interviewee and encourages communication. Like gestures, eye contact works to control the flow of conversation. Most people look away for a few seconds before they finish speaking; they look back just as they conclude, signaling that it is the other person's turn to speak (Davis 1975). Used properly, eye contact is effective in establishing and maintaining communication.

If you are a dominant, assertive individual, be careful how you use eye contact. You don't want to frighten interviewees with your eye contact pattern. Do not stare at the interviewee; this creates undue stress, which may interfere with communication. Be sure to give the interviewee time to think clearly without trying to stare the person down (Drake 1972, p. 86).

Touch

Touching another human being in a gentle, reassuring way indicates concern, warmth, and closeness. At times, it is helpful to place your hand gently on the interviewee's hand, arm, or shoulder. A reassuring touch strengthens the bonds of rapport. Proficient interviewers learn to use reassuring touch to exhibit their acceptance of the interviewee and to strengthen interpersonal communication. When it seems fitting, your touch can be an integral part of an interview, signaling a special caring inexpressible through words.

A complicated combination of things occurs when two people touch, however, so be careful to determine whether it is appropriate to touch a particular interviewee. Not everyone will allow touching to take place. Hostile or extremely reluctant interviewees will usually not allow themselves to be touched, sometimes not even to shake hands. Many interviewees sense their personal space as an extension of their ego and will go to almost any length to preserve it. They do not want others to come close to them, and they certainly do not want to be touched by anyone. This restraint usually has nothing to do with you personally and probably has nothing to do with the matter under investigation.

Positive Silence

The tactic of silence can be a weapon for battle or a marvelous instrument of the most delicate construction. Improperly used, the interviewer's silence is a form of authoritarian punishment. The "silent treatment" is the ultimate form of rejection and a sure sign of the interviewer's displeasure (Bennis et al. 1973, p. 78). The use of abusive silence is a self-defeating tactic that often offends the interviewee, builds tension, and reduces cooperation (Drake 1972, p. 85). Unless employed subtly, your silence may be equated with withdrawal, rejection, disapproval, or an implied threat. Silence shakes up interviewees when it occurs repeatedly.

When used appropriately, however, without an intentional threat to the interviewee, silence can strengthen rapport and encourage compliance. You can use a positive silence to indicate your acceptance of the interviewee or to signal your control of the interview. Interviewees can sense the mood of the moment, the implicit meaning of the interviewer's silence. I support using silence to keep the pot bubbling, not to antagonize or alienate interviewees. It can be a constructive part of your tactics and need not be a harsh method.

Keep your questions simple and direct, and wait after asking each question to give the interviewee time to construct a thoughtful reply (Dexter 1970, p. 112). A brief silence or pause after the interviewee finishes speaking can be used to indicate that more is expected in response to the question. When I pause between questions, I find that interviewees often provide further information to fill the silence (Drake 1972, p. 86). A positive silence thus produces meaningful and relevant information that would not be available from a fast-moving interview (Drake 1972, p. 85). Research indicates that "there is positive correlation between the amount of silence used by the interviewer and the interviewee's general level of spontaneity" (Gorden 1969, p. 188). When I choose to use silence as a tactic, I glance at the interviewee rather than stare. Staring can be oppressive when coupled with silence; silence alone is enough to bring out meaningful tension in the interviewee. It is sometimes helpful to introduce silence when the interviewee least expects it.

As useful a tactic as positive silence is, some interviewees can withstand it. Experienced, composed interviewees handle silence by sitting patiently and expectantly or by asking questions to distract you from your efforts. Some interviewees handle silence by returning the interviewer's stare with a calm, anticipatory look. Others counter with their own silence in the hopes of revealing the interviewer's tension or lack of confidence. The skill of interviewees in handling silence is a sign of their ability to control distress. Hence, it is beneficial to try to gauge an interviewee's skill in this regard.

Interviewees who resent your authority may engage in long intervals of silence before answering your questions (Davis 1975).

Interviewees who have a poor self-image, who feel inadequate and helpless, may use silence to express their annoyance, resentment, or anger. They may engage in lengthy pauses, sudden silences, and an unexplained inability to discuss pertinent detail (Woody and Woody 1972, p. 163). Many interviewees resent being interrupted when speaking. Some can become so petulant, impatient, or irritable that they refuse to talk at all. Interviewees who realize that silence makes the questioner uncomfortable and may intentionally use it to trap the interviewer into proceeding before they have answered the question (Benjamin 1974, p. 25; Gorden 1969).

Inexperienced interviewers sometimes have a low tolerance for silence and become distressed by it. For anxious interviewers who lack self-confidence, a brief period of silence may seem almost endless. However, the interviewee's silence is not necessarily a hindrance (Woody and Woody 1972, p. 166), and it need not disrupt the interviewer's strategy. Through training and practice, interviewers can learn to tolerate quiet in an interview and to use it to maximum advantage. Even if the interviewee's silence makes you feel uneasy, opposed, or thwarted, it is vital that you not respond in an aggressive manner. Don't respond to the silence as if it were a personal attack on you (Benjamin 1974, p. 25). It is equally important that you not suggest responses to your questions. When I sense that interviewees are trying to use silence to their advantage, I assume that they are also using other ploys to try to manipulate me. These formidable competitors need special attention, closer observation, and more careful assessment. Truthful, straightforward, compliant interviewees do not employ tactics of strategic silence.

REVIEW QUESTIONS

1. How does the interviewer act as a catalyst during an interview?

2. What is rapport?

3. When should you begin to develop rapport during an interview?

4. What are the advantages of establishing rapport?

5. Are you approving of the crime when you are friendly to the criminal?

6. How might you go about building rapport?

7. How can you tell if a silent interviewee is truly listening?

8. Why doesn't the use of sarcasm, ridicule, or cynicism help you gain cooperation?

9. What is role reversal, and how should it be handled?

10. How should you end an unproductive interview?

11. What is active listening?

12. What does it take to be a "perfect listener"?

13. How can you show that you are paying attention to the interviewee?

14. What are the consequences of inattention during an interview?

15. Why is it important to concentrate during an interview?

16. How can you signal your acceptance of the interviewee?

17. What is detachment, and how can you use it?

18. Why is patience a virtue for interviewers?

19. How can you use body language to signal positive messages?

20. How does eye contact help control the flow of conversation?

21. When is it okay to touch an interviewee?

22. How can you use silence in positive ways?

23. How shouldn't you respond to an interviewee's silence?

7

Authority and Neutrality in the Investigative Interview

Typically, an authority figure functions as a representative of some organization or entity. As difficult as it may seem, an investigator is most successful maintaining a middle ground—balancing on the tight rope of neutrality. An investigator's loyalty is to the organization he or she represents, but it can be extremely helpful to the success of an inquiry if this connection is clouded over and not too clearly discernible.

AUTHORITY AND POWER

In its simplest form, power is the ability to control, influence, or cause others to do what you want them to do (*Effective Uses of Power and Authority* 1980). It can be expressed negatively or positively. Authority is the vested, or conveyed, right to exercise power over others. It is the right to command, to enforce laws, to exact obedience, to determine, or to judge, and its basis may be legal, traditional, or social. For example, as an FBI agent, I was vested with specific responsibilities to act on behalf of the United States government. To a large extent, my behavior was dictated by the Constitution and the rules and regulations of the FBI. As an authority figure, I functioned within these guidelines, but beyond the guidelines, I set my own personal standards of operation in dealing with people. Investigators wield the authority granted them by virtue of their position, and they function on behalf of a segment of the community (Bennis et al. 1973, p. 62). As with all positions of authority, there is an organization establishing guidelines that impact investigators' behavior. Each investigator then functions based on personal ethics, and no matter which organization investigators represent, they are personally responsible for how they command, determine avenues of inquiry, and judge outcomes. Because the misuse of their authority carries serious potential consequences, investigators have a great responsibility to exercise their power thoughtfully.

Some investigators wrongly consider power to be a permanent possession. In fact, legitimate power emanates from the role or position that the investigator holds. When used positively in an interview, authority promotes confidence and accomplishment, boosting the interviewee's self-esteem and encouraging his or her cooperation.

The Misuse of Authority

Some interviewers exercise their authority aggressively all the time, rather than assertively and only when necessary. These authoritarians demand absolute obedience without regard for the individual rights of others (Bennis et al. 1973). When crossed, they become intolerant. They threaten interviewees, describing the steps they will take if the interviewee does not cooperate. Arrogantly passing judgment, authoritarians humiliate interviewees, stripping them of their self-respect. They expect to be treated like gods, and often are, because of the power they hold to affect the lives of others. Power misusers lack an awareness of their real selves. They are corrupt, prejudiced, sadistic opportunists exploiting their position of power to earn the respect of their peers (Adorno et al. 1950).

Authoritarians wield their power in such a way as to make interviewees feel helpless, impotent, and fearful, forcing them on the defensive (Bennis et al. 1973, p. 252). The investigator's superior attitude tells interviewees that the investigator is not seeking a problem-solving relationship, that their help is not desired, and that it is likely that their power, status, or worth will be reduced if they cooperate in the investigation (Bennis et al. 1973, p. 492). The result is resistance. If the investigator responds aggressively to resistance, someone may get hurt. The modulated use of power is the only legal and civilized tactic.

The more you understand about what is happening in the interview, the more likely it is that you will respond in a constructive manner (OSS Assessment Staff 1948, p. 171). We all act in accordance with our own individual reasoning power; we tend to invent plausible explanations, or rationalizations, for our acts (Nierenberg 1968). Typically, interviewees use rationalization to preserve their self-image (Berg and Bass 1961, p. 252). Your use of power in any form may provoke the interviewee to behave defensively (Woody and Woody 1972, p. 170). Anxiety does not promote compliance. Therefore, avoid entering into a power struggle with interviewees; this will only lead to alienation (Nirenberg 1963).

The Positive Application of Authority

The authoritarian interviewer's negative use of power arises from his or her feelings of insecurity and inadequacy. Proficient interviewers, on the other hand, use power in positive ways as they strive toward personal growth and self-affirmation. They are empowered with self-appreciation, vision, and purpose. Personal motivation is based upon the principle that you are the end result of what you want to be. Success comes from inner strength, conscious willpower, and an unwavering determination to succeed. With these you can develop courage, enthusiasm, confidence, and belief in your own ability.

When the needs of interview participants clash, develop a strategy to use to your advantage, applying referent power, the power of your position that symbolizes the organization you work for, in subtle ways. To argue with the interviewee is self-defeating, as is running away. For interviewees, information is power. Faced with a threatening authoritarian, interviewees rarely see any constructive advantage to giving up what little power they retain. You should be willing to subtly and indirectly reach a point of agreement where some of the interviewee's needs are met. Interviewees may willingly provide information in return for assurances of confidentiality, protection, or some other concession.

Interviewees who have been pushed, pressured, bribed, or overpowered by parents or other authority figures may be guarded, extremely uncomfortable, or uncooperative during an interview. Don't take the interviewee's resistance personally. You may merely be a handy authority figure for the interviewee to lash out at. Try to suggest subtly that power returns to those who decide to comply.

The interviewing techniques suggested in this book are intended to encourage your use of positive authority in everything you do—from the tone of your voice to the way you actively listen. Although you may, to some degree, be insecure and self-consciousness in your behavior, your human interaction skills will improve with practice. It is too easy to use harsh, abrasive methods. If you strengthen your willpower, you will not be easily drawn into destructive behavior.

THE VALUE OF RESTRAINED AUTHORITY

This case, involving an eight-year-old girl who was reportedly molested by a thirty-seven-year-old family friend, illustrates what a skilled investigator can do. If a child's verbal skills and maturity preclude legal cross-examination, other reasonable proof of the accusation is needed. Although anyone under age fourteen, in my view, is not usually suitable as a polygraph examinee, I recommend using a polygraph to gather additional information in the inquiry.

With her parents and a female social worker present, a male law enforcement investigator interviewed the child. The following extract is from the tape-recorded interview.

> **Question 75:** What happened?
> **Child:** It sorta hurted when I did.
> **Q76:** It did? Did it sting?
> **Child:** No.
> **Q77:** Okay, how did it hurt? Can you describe it?
> **Child:** Well it sorta did sting.
> **Q78:** Okay, did you tell your mom that?
> **Child:** I just told her it hurted when I went to the bathroom.
> **Q79:** Has it ever hurted like that before when you went to the bathroom?
> **Child:** Yeah.
> **Q80:** Was there a reason why it hurted like that before?
> **Child:** Uh-huh.

Although the child did not use proper grammar in response to questions 75 and 78, the interviewer did not correct her. To help cement a close relationship, the investigator even repeated the child's terminology in questions 79 and 80. No doubt the child heard how the investigator worded the question and on some level of awareness felt closer to him. We can only imagine how the child might have felt if the investigator had corrected her.

NEUTRALITY

True professionals never collect evidence to suit some preconceived notion of who is culpable. To be a successful interviewer, you should approach all investigations (and all interviewees) with a floating point strategy and an open mind. Collect all available evidence fairly and impartially, and allow it to lead you to a logical conclusion.

THE VALUE OF KEEPING AN OPEN MIND

It is human nature to draw conclusions prematurely, basing them on preconceived notions and the opinions of others. However, the experienced investigator disregards the opinions of others, making up his or her mind based upon available evidence.

In an embezzlement case I looked into, I was advised not to waste my time investigating a particular midmanagement employee. He was slated for big things with the company and was highly trusted. He was not in any way considered a suspect, I was told. Other employees were suggested as the main players responsible for the company's losses.

During the investigation, I obtained a confession in which the thief revealed that he had sold stolen merchandise to the favored midmanager. Skeptically, I arranged for the confessed thief to meet the midmanager and discuss how he had told all in the confession. I later confronted the favored employee, and he admitted receiving stolen company property.

Encourage the interviewee's compliance by deliberately establishing your neutrality (Dexter 1970, p. 25). Keep all of your remarks neutral, avoiding a critical or judgmental stance (Kahn and Cannell 1957). You might even give the impression that you are, ever so slightly, leaning toward the interviewee's side. It is important to demonstrate respect for all interviewees and an awareness of their need for security (Kahn and Cannell 1957, p. 126).

Interview subjects can generally tell your "party line" by your opening words (Bennis et al. 1973, p. 490). It takes but a few moments, a few words, a few nonverbal signals to reveal your relative position—that is, your opinion of the interviewee. A biased or judgmental demeanor may adversely affect the outcome of the interview and may limit your investigative progress (Dexter 1970, p. 150).

Do not conduct the interview in an accusatory way; instead, keep yourself open, positive, and neutral. Do not reveal any suspicions you might have of the interviewee's truthfulness or innocence until the time is right to do so. Especially when you want someone to undergo a detection-of-deception exam or other test, it is important to adopt a neutral, wait-and-see stance. The tension associated with the test may be enough to interfere with the interviewee's clear thinking, causing him or her to refuse to cooperate. Don't make matters worse with an accusatory attitude.

While remaining neutral and objective in your methods, do not give interviewees a way of relieving tensions easily, except through verbal expression. Encourage them to evaluate their situation on its real merits rather than be guided by anxiety, irritation, or other emotions (Nirenberg 1963). Criminal victims and witnesses may allow their feelings and emotions to cloud the facts, distorting the information you seek. Do your best to lead interviewees from emotional responses to factual responses based upon clear thinking (Maltz 1960).

Do not allow the interviewee's mood to upset your own composure (Nirenberg 1963). Be prepared to put up with a certain amount of verbal abuse from rebellious interviewees. Your neutral stance when explaining how the interviewee can assist in your inquiry is vital to your success.

Signaling Your Neutrality

Interviewees can pick up on subtle signals that belie your claims of neutrality. It is nearly impossible for interviewers to eliminate the effects of prejudice, hate, and other emotions on their behavior. However, they can control the expression of their personal views and values to avoid destroying their chances of obtaining the interviewee's cooperation (Wicks and Josephs 1972).

Presenting a neutral facade is a difficult task. Regardless of the hat you wear, interviewees may suspect some hidden objective or ulterior motive. Hence, you should do your best to avoid displaying negative signals during an interview. Many comments can be negative or positive in character, depending on how they are voiced. Saying "Please go on" with the wrong intonation might stop the flow of information. Your tone of voice may signal that you are biased, not neutral, causing a breakdown in communication.

Your tone of voice, facial expressions, language, and timing must all be congruent with your claim of neutrality. If by force, volume, or tone of voice you emphasize certain consequences, the interviewee will quickly decide that you're hoping to hear a particular response. Consequences imply an either-or situation, such as, "If you don't do such and such, then . . ." If you repeatedly call attention to a particular set of consequences, or if you react to an interviewee's focus on the positive consequences by quickly switching to a discussion of the negative consequences, you may be perceived as being less than neutral (Binder and Price 1977, p. 172).

Making an Accusation

Why would an interviewee talk openly with an investigator who seems to be judgmental, critical, or skeptical? You will find that it is difficult to keep your personal views and your suspicions hidden, but doing so is vital to the progress of your inquiry. Don't be too quick to provide an opinion regarding the interviewee's veracity. Don't make your suspicions known until you are reasonably certain of your facts. Interviewees who sense that you have prematurely concluded that they're lying will become defensive. When you have been convinced by the available evidence, when revealing your conclusion will help you collect more evidence, that is the time to do it. Reserve your opinion until then.

REVIEW QUESTIONS

1. Define *power* and *authority*.

2. Why must investigators exercise their power thoughtfully?

3. Describe some tactics used by authoritarians.

4. What message does the investigator's superior attitude send to the interviewee?

5. What does information represent to the interviewee, and why might he or she be reluctant to share it?

6. Why do some people resist authority?

7. Is it possible for the investigator to hold all of the power in an interview? If so, would this be a good idea? Explain.

8. Why should investigators keep an open mind when beginning an investigation?

9. How can investigators adopt a neutral attitude?

10. How can the investigator avoid displaying negative nonverbal signals during the interview?

8

The Self-Fulfilling Prophecy

The self-fulfilling prophecy is based on the notion that expectation produces the reality; that is, we achieve what we expect to achieve. The self-fulfilling prophecy has a profound effect on interpersonal communication. According to Dr. Raymond L. Gorden, "One of the important forces in social interaction is the tendency for one person to communicate, verbally and nonverbally, his expectations to another person. The second person then tends to respond consciously or unconsciously to those expectations. This may be viewed as one manifestation of the more general human tendency to conform to a group of peers and to the suggestion of higher status persons in society" (Gorden 1969, p. 84). Industrial psychologists have long recognized the necessity of creating management patterns that foster motivation, improve communication, and increase productivity. Case studies show that high expectations lead to high performance and that low expectations result in poor performance. Definite social and psychological processes are involved in the self-fulfilling prophecy; the power of positive thinking and magic are not, according to educator and psychologist Robert K. Merton. Evidence from recognized authors emphasizes the benefits of applying the self-fulfilling prophecy.[1]

We can apply the self-fulfilling prophecy to investigative interviews. The expectations with which we approach interviewing will tend to be realized. Our attitude toward interviewees determines how we treat them, and this, in turn, influences how they behave. If you expect to uncover the truth in your investigations, treat your interview subjects as though they want to provide you with truthful information—and most of them will. Try to act in a pleasant, friendly, and encouraging manner to help the interviewee think clearly. Unintentional communication can be incredibly subtle and complex in both negative and positive ways. Many interviews are like a parent talking to a child because of their emotionally tense character. Hence, try to recognize and comprehend emotions that could produce fears and anxieties that interrupt or restrict clear thinking.

The self-fulfilling prophecy is commonly referred to as the Pygmalion effect, and it relates directly to the Galatea effect. Both are based upon expectations. The Galatea effect refers to the expectations we place on ourselves. Self-expectations are an intrinsic part of making our dreams a reality. It takes courage to discover what we can achieve (*Empowerment Series* 1992). We must work hard and commit ourselves to our goals if we are to succeed. Unfortunately, the Galatea effect can be negated by the expectations others have of us.

While applying the Pygmalion effect (SFP) during investigations, it is vital to understand the requirements and meet the expectations of those we investigate. It takes extraordinary drive and determination to be successful as you commit yourself to greater proficiency. Productivity and personal development are the goals.

---

[1]The following authors cite evidence supporting the self-fulfilling prophecy: Rensis Likert, J. Sterling Livingston, Douglas Murray McGregor, Robert K. Merton, and Robert Rosenthal.

The Pygmalion effect, on the other hand, refers to the expectations we have of others and they have of us. Playwright George Bernard Shaw illustrated the self-fulfilling prophecy in the play *Pygmalion*, which was adapted as the musical *My Fair Lady*. In this play, Eliza, a flower girl from the slums of London, insists that she cannot become the lady Professor Higgins is training her to be until he *sees* her as a lady, instead of as a flower girl masquerading as a lady. Eliza says, "You see, really and truly, apart from the things anyone can pick up [the dressing, the proper way of speaking, and so on], the difference between a lady and a flower girl is not how she behaves, but how she's treated. I shall always be a flower girl to Professor Higgins, because he always treats me as a flower girl, and always will, but I know I can be a lady to you, because you always treat me as a lady, and always will" (Shaw 1994; Yeschke 1993, p. 61).

Clearly, how we behave toward an individual influences that person's response. Everything we do and say conveys our expectations. Far more than verbal prodding, the self-fulfilling prophecy encompasses your total behavior, conscious and subconscious. Let's look more closely at this theoretical concept and how it can work for you.

THE FOUR ELEMENTS OF THE SELF-FULFILLING PROPHECY

In his dissertation, educator and psychologist Robert Rosenthal showed through scientific experiments that "the power of expectation alone" significantly influences the behavior of others. Drawing on his experience as a teacher, he showed that if he believed that the students in his experiments had greater potential, and if this belief raised his expectations of them, and if he transmitted his expectations to the students, then, as a result, they became higher achievers. Through studies and experiments, Rosenthal and his associates developed a theory about how expectations can be communicated. They broke the theory down into four elements: climate, feedback, input, and output

(*Productivity and the Self-Fulfilling Prophecy* 1975). We will define and describe each element below, but remember that each is an integral part of the whole.

Element 1: Climate

The climate communicates positive or negative expectations to others through nonverbal messages, from body language to paralanguage. Body language includes mannerisms, gestures, eye contact, facial expression, and body posture. Paralanguage encompasses tone of voice and the use of silence. The climate of an interview is in play from the beginning to the end of the encounter. Before you even have a chance to speak, you are under scrutiny for signs of acceptance and trust.

Some interviewers are adept at using the climate of an interview to allay the interviewee's fears and to encourage cooperation. Others can use climate by reading, talking to and observing skillful interviewers, and practicing on everyone with whom they come in contact. In the interview itself, the deliberate communication of nonverbal messages requires subtle delivery to avoid the appearance of pretense and to avoid arousing the interviewee's suspicions.

Element 2: Feedback

Feedback refers to "the process of correction through incorporation of information about [the] effects [of one's performance]. When a person perceives the results produced by his own actions, the information so derived will influence subsequent actions. Feedback thus becomes a steering device upon which learning and the correction of errors are based" (Reusch and Kees 1954, p. 4). Investigators reveal their expectations to the interviewee in their response to the interviewee's feedback. This response is an ongoing process, encompassing both verbal and nonverbal communication. It is difficult to anticipate feedback from interviewees. Therefore, carefully prepare yourself to meet and handle the unexpected. Stay alert, neutral, flexible, and professional. You can channel feedback by emphasizing your input.

Element 3: Input

Input is the verbal transmittal of the investigator's expectations to the interviewee. It is the key ingredient of any interview. Interviewees continually read verbal and nonverbal input and interpret it relative to their own situation. Prepare your verbal input to establish a clear picture of what you expect from the interviewee. The goal is to set the stage so that it is virtually impossible for the interviewee to surprise or divert you. Your neutral stance in explaining how the interviewee can assist your inquiry is vital to your success.

Element 4: Output

Output is the response from the interviewee. It might be silence, uncooperative behavior, lies, or truthful information. The interviewer communicates his or her expectations of the interviewee's output and encourages or discourages cooperation. If the revelation of the truth is the desired output, it is helpful to develop a positive, humane interaction style that encourages interviewees to comply. Treating interviewees as though they want to provide the greatest degree of truthful cooperation establishes a high probability that they will do so.

APPLYING THE SELF-FULFILLING PROPHECY

I have used the self-fulfilling prophecy in interviews and interrogations throughout my professional career. Before every interaction, I take stock of myself and my overall expectations. During this mental exercise, I remind myself that I am a talented and resourceful individual capable of handling a wide variety of inquiries ranging from murder to counterespionage. I remind myself that this new investigation is much like the others I have handled. I consider what I expect of myself and how I intend to treat the interviewee. Before even knowing the details of the new inquiry, I establish a personal, private strategy and determine to do the best professional job I can. This helps me set my course and focus my energy.

Your belief in yourself and your expectation of success should exist side by side before each interview, regardless of the investigative circumstances. Belief and expectation are an integral part of the investigator's being, a basic part of his or her philosophical makeup. With experience, successful investigators become more and more aware of their influence on the outcome of investigations. Skill in using belief and expectation gradually builds over years of experience. A true test of that skill is in its application—that is, in how you subtly influence others to comply with your requests for information. There are two practical steps you can take toward acquiring this skill—one intellectual, the other practical:

- Mental belief and expectation. Believe in yourself and your ability to verbally and nonverbally encourage others to provide truthful information. Believe that the interviewee is ready, willing, and able to share truthful information. Maintain a positive expectation of success. Have faith in your abilities. With everything that you think, do, and say, demonstrate that you anticipate that the interviewee will cooperate.

- Applied action. How you treat others greatly determines their response to you. Therefore, express an "I'm okay, you're okay" attitude. Treat each interviewee as having value as a human being, regardless of the inquiry. People tend to live up to your expectations of them. If your tactics are positive, the interviewee will probably cooperate with your investigation; if negative, they will probably, to some degree, refuse to cooperate.

When applying the self-fulfilling prophecy during investigations, it is vital to understand the needs and meet the expectations of those you investigate. (See Chapter 2.) The self-fulfilling prophecy draws its power from the need of interview participants to be recognized as worthwhile individuals. It is fueled by people's tendency to behave in ways consistent with their self-concept as well as with others' expectations.

How can investigators demonstrate an accepting attitude when dealing with a particularly heinous crime like child molestation? It's certainly not easy. My suggestion is to pretend that you are playing a role in the theater. Make your performance believable. Avoid being noticeably judgmental. Find some value in each interviewee, and don't allow yourself to condemn the person outwardly. As repulsive as this may seem, assist the subject to rationalize his or her involvement in the crime. In a child molestation case, for example, the abuser may want to believe that the child seduced him or her. Go along with this; disguise your contempt. If he or she senses that you are not neutral, you may not obtain a confession or an admission. To uncover the truth, you may need to temporarily modify your methods or your thinking to obtain the necessary cooperation. That is, you may have to do or say things that you might normally find objectionable. This is tough to do, no doubt, but it is necessary if you are to be of the greatest service to your community.

Presenting Expectations Subtly

Present your positive expectations of the interviewee's cooperation subtly. Don't actually say, "I know you want to tell me . . ." Just treat interviewees as though they want to comply. In reality, interviewees often do not want to cooperate with an investigation—at least not at first and not to the extent that you expect. By acting on a false assumption, however—that each interviewee will want to cooperate—you turn your expectation into reality. You can persuade interview suspects to accept the idea of compliance even though they had no such interest at first. Sell them on the idea in subtle, thought-provoking, legal ways.

Applying the Galatea Effect

The Galatea effect is a boost in personal performance that is based upon self-efficacy—the investigator's judgment of his or her capabilities. This self-efficacy is based on belief, motivation, and performance, and in turn, influences the performance standard you select for yourself. Self-efficacy is not so much to do with the skills you have but your judgment of what you can do with your skills. Self-efficacy arises primarily from the effects of mastery, modeling, and persuasion. That is, self-efficacy is influenced by personal accomplishment, watching others succeed, and being persuaded by yourself and others that you can perform to high standards.

While self-confidence in one's skills is built primarily upon having successfully used these skills in the past, you can also build your skills by watching the behavior of others who are successful and listening to their advice. At first, self-efficacy is task-specific and emanates from the individual's belief that he or she can perform a particular task at a specific level of competence. An important variable in predicting success is an individual's confidence that he or she can master new investigative situations (Gist 1987; Eden and Kinnar 1991). As your experience builds, self-efficacy emanates from your success marked by self-administered rewards. Rewards reinforce accomplishment. If you expect to successfully conclude an investigation, and you then do, it's a good idea to reward yourself in some way. Some reward such as buying yourself an ice cream cone will be a symbolic pat on the back for a job well done. Once established, self-efficacy applies to all investigative situations. Set your goals, observe others, expect positive outcomes, and self-monitor your performance (Gist 1987; Eden and Kinnar 1991).

REVIEW QUESTIONS

1. On what idea is the self-fulfilling prophecy based?

2. What is the impact of expectations on performance?

3. How does your attitude toward interviewees influence their behavior?

4. Compare the Galatea effect and the Pygmalion effect.

5. How can you convey your expectations?

6. What are the four elements of the self-fulfilling prophecy, and how does each relate to investigative interviewing?

7. How can you maintain an accepting attitude when investigating heinous crimes?

8. How can you demonstrate that you expect cooperation?

9. What influences the development of self-efficacy?

10. How can you gain greater confidence and proficiency as an investigator?

9

Overview of the Interview Process

In this chapter, we will review the different stages of the interview process and learn how to apply some of the tactical concepts discussed earlier in this book. You are encouraged to use these tactics to think about interviewing in new ways. There is an interplay among the stages, approaches, and intensity levels of the interview process, as the polyphasic flowchart (Figure 9.1) shows. These categories will take on more meaning as we proceed, but for now, allow the flowchart to serve as a road map for the interview process.

THE HISTORICAL PHASE

The historical phase of the interview process begins long before the investigator and interviewee ever meet. It covers all of the attitudes and beliefs that the participants bring to the interview. These influences were learned, directly or indirectly, from our

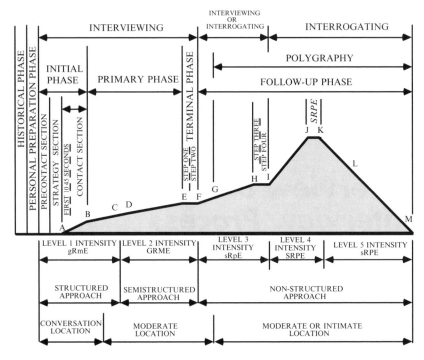

Figure 9.1   A polyphasic flowchart showing the stages of the investigative interview.

parents or caregivers in childhood and were picked up from other sources throughout life. Some of us carry a great deal of garbage in our intellectual and emotional "baggage," including biases and prejudices that hamper our productivity and effectiveness.

Undoubtedly, our emotional baggage influences and shapes our behavior during the interview process. Don't overlook or underestimate the importance of the historical phase. The more self-awareness you bring to the interview, the more effective you will be in the personal preparation phase.

THE PERSONAL PREPARATION PHASE

All adults have the opportunity to modify the biases and negative attitudes they learned while growing up. As investigators, we can take a close look at ourselves and change those things about us that have a negative impact on the process of communication. In our personal rebuilding, we can pilot our abilities to use the positive interview tactics suggested in this book. It is up to us to look in our emotional baggage and modify its contents if necessary. If we take the opportunity to discard much of the garbage, we will lead healthier lives. Through education, training, and experience, we can discard our biases and prejudices and become more proficient and effective investigators.

As we have seen, biases and prejudices lead to misguided observation, evaluation, and assessment, so professionals don't knowingly bring them into their inquiries. They acknowledge that how they treat people is greatly influenced by their past, but nevertheless, they remain in control of their own behavior.

All investigators are not equally talented in how they handle human interactions, but all interviewers can be applied scientists, discriminating among variables and using systematic, purposeful investigative methods. Investigators demonstrate their professional adaptability through their willingness to modify their behavior in a never-ending learning process. Their ethical behavior reveals itself as competence and leadership. Figure 9.2 provides another road map of the interview process, one that illustrates the thoughts and emotions behind the different stages.

THE INITIAL PHASE

The fundamental purpose of the initial phase of the interview process is to consider detailed information regarding the incident under investigation, the people who might be involved, and the conditions under which the interviews will take place. The initial phase consists of three sections: precontact, strategic planning, and contact. The third section covers the first few critical minutes of each interview. We will discuss each section in turn.

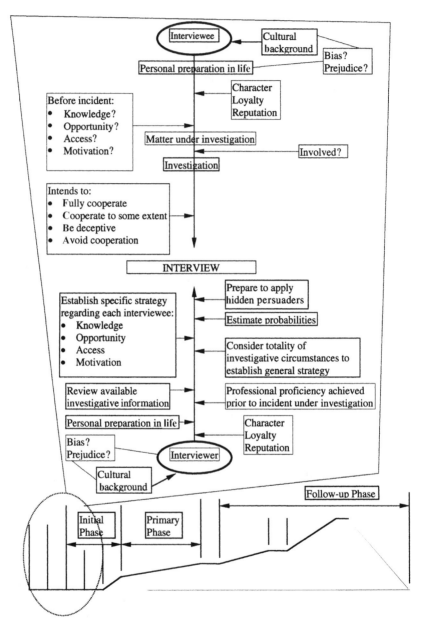

Figure 9.2   Elements affecting human interaction in the investigative interview. The life experiences of both the investigator and the interviewee come into play during the interview.

Precontact

During precontact (Figure 9.3), the interviewer becomes familiar with the available information about the matter under investigation and the various suspects and begins to formulate a flexible interview plan. This plan includes a clear picture of the objectives of the interview and a floating-point strategy.

The Floating-Point Strategy

Investigations are often based on probability and likelihood, and estimating the probability that a particular person committed the crime is the essence of the floating-point strategy (FPS). The FPS is a flexible problem-solving process that can be used in all inquiries. The investigator applies the FPS as soon as most of the elements of the investigative problem are known. The FPS allows the investigator to reevaluate and, if necessary, modify his or her operating hypothesis as new evidence is uncovered. Picture the problem-solving process as having numerous points at which you can reevaluate your progress and determine whether you are on the right track. Your strategy floats from point to point, never becoming fixed until you are reasonably sure of your assessment of the evidence.

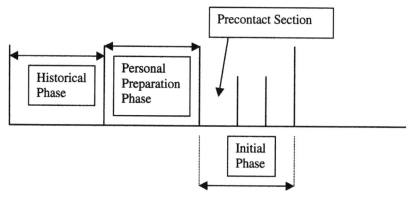

Figure 9.3   The precontact section of the initial phase. This is the time when the investigator gathers information about both the matter under investigation and the suspects.

The Preliminary Inquiry

During the precontact section, the investigator collects evidence and reviews information collected from victims and witnesses. The success of an investigation is often based on how thoroughly the investigator gathers this preliminary data. Specific details about the incident form the foundation to which the investigator will refer throughout the investigation. Clues about motivation may be found in the lifestyle, habits, hobbies, stressors, and needs of the suspects. Be careful when conducting the preliminary inquiry! The person who provides the preliminary information in an investigation may have a hidden agenda—a plan to deceive you and mislead you by providing false information. Look for the telltale signs of deception: inconsistencies, illogical details, information clouded by fear or anger. Watch for calculated attempts to obscure the facts.

Strategic Planning

Experienced investigators make interviewing look easier than it is. The novice interviewer may watch the casual performance of the experienced interviewer and incorrectly assume the relaxed prevailing emotional tone or attitude of the experienced interviewer indicates no important or noticeable research or planning. In fact, strategic planning, the second section of the initial phase, is an important part of the interview process (Figure 9.4). During this section, the investigator evaluates potential interviewees, prepares an interview strategy based on what he or she has learned, and prepares psychologically for the interview.

Evaluating Potential Interviewees

Before conducting any interviews, the investigator evaluates each potential interviewee, based on information provided by those close to the investigation. The investigator then calculates the chances of gaining truthful testimonial evidence from that person.

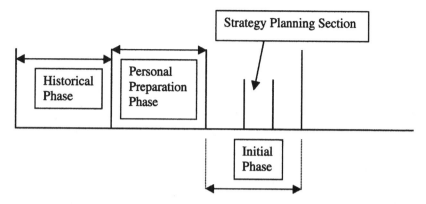

Figure 9.4 The strategic planning section of the initial phase. During this phase, the investigator considers all aspects of the planned interviews, including where they will be held and in what order the suspects will be interviewed.

This calculation is a subjective estimate—nothing more than thoughts about whether someone will be easy or hard to interview. The investigator also considers how well he or she will get along with each interviewee and how cooperative that person will be. As you prepare for an investigation, you will probably need to evaluate potential interviewees sight unseen, based on the preliminary information you are given.

Creating an Interview Strategy

The goal of an investigative interview is to gain as much truthful information as possible. You want interviewees to tell you everything they know about the matter under investigation. Interviewees have the power of information—information you need to conclude the investigation successfully. As discussed earlier, many factors determine whether interviewees decide to relinquish or hold on to this information. It is important, therefore, to plan an appropriate strategy for each interview. It is better to be overprepared than underprepared, especially when dealing with people who may try to deceive you (Quinn and Zunin 1972).

Interviewees are selected on the basis of their knowledge, opportunity, access, and motivation related to the matter under investigation. Planning for an interview might include conducting a background check of the interviewee. Having advance information about the interviewee allows the investigator to anticipate whether the person will cooperate and helps the investigator prepare an appropriate strategy for the interview. Awareness of interviewees' attitudes and feelings can help you mold yourself to meet their personalities and counter potential reluctance. Preparing for reluctance is vital, though you should always expect compliance. In most instances, though, the investigator has little or no specific knowledge about potential interviewees before beginning an investigation.

Before conducting an interview, plan how you will behave during the encounter. How will you speak, and how will you act? How will you show energy, strength, and concentration? To what extent will you review details with the interviewee? Will your review of details help the interviewee remember additional information? How will you encourage the interviewee to be truthful? If your encouragement is inspired with courage, spirit, and confidence, you will probably gain pertinent and helpful information.

Preparing Psychologically for the Interview

Plan to enter each interview with an open mind. This means not only keeping your mind open to the guilt or innocence of each suspect, but being accepting and nonjudgmental, even when you are interacting with those whom you have designated prime suspects. In addition, be determined to put misinformation aside and think for yourself. Don't accept any piece of information until you have evaluated it in light of the other evidence.

Use positive expectation in all efforts to gather information. In other words, treat interviewees as though they want to comply. In everything you do and say, act as though you know the interviewee truly wants to cooperate with the investigation. Most interviewees do, in fact, respond positively to this expectation. (See Chapter 8.)

Positive behavior is necessary if you are to achieve proficiency as an interviewer. Excellent interviewers modify their behavior to inspire and convince interviewees to provide truthful information, and with sufficient practice and dedication, many develop into capable interrogators. By applying honed interviewing skills and focusing your energies on improvement, you will become competent at solving complicated investigative problems. It's not force, but finesse that counts in human interaction.

Contact

Points A and B of the polyphasic flowchart (see Figure 9.1) define the first four minutes of the actual interview. Thus span of time is the contact section of the initial phase (Figure 9.5). Your main purpose during these first four minutes is to establish a rapport with the interviewee (see Chapter 6). Also during this time, you will begin using the tactics referred to as *hidden persuaders* (see box). You will continue to use these tactics throughout the interview, even into the follow-up phase, when inconsistencies are resolved, confrontation takes place, and admissions and confessions are sought and obtained.

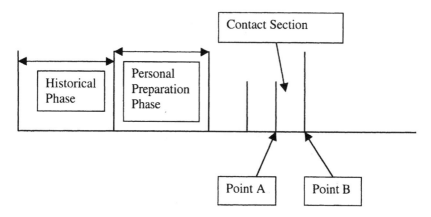

Figure 9.5   The contact section of the initial phase (the first four minutes of each interview). The investigator and the interviewee have their first verbal and nonverbal exchanges during this time.

THE HIDDEN PERSUADERS

Throughout your career, you will learn to use certain tactics when gathering information during an interview. For example, you will learn to build rapport with the interviewee, to maintain a positive attitude, and to listen actively. I call these tactics the *hidden persuaders*. They are so-called because they help the interviewer display favorable characteristics and screen out less favorable ones. They are designed to show the interviewee that the interviewer can be trusted. If they are applied sensitively and skillfully, they will have significant and positive effects on the outcome of your interviews.

In most interviews, the investigator has at least one hidden agenda, some unannounced reason for conducting the interview. For example, one hidden agenda when interviewing a victim is to determine whether a crime actually took place. The practiced use of the hidden persuaders will help conceal the interviewer's true agenda and will help the investigator outsmart the interviewee.

- Consider the human needs of interview participants.
- Build and maintain rapport.
- Use a positive attitude.
- Apply flexible methods.
- Cover suspiciousness.
- Use creative imagination.
- Apply the self-fulfilling prophecy.
- Exhibit human warmth, sensitivity, empathy, respect, and genuineness.
- Use nonjudgmental acceptance.
- Listen actively and attentively.
- Be patient.

- Be positive: Use positive silence, positive eye contact, positive personal space (proxemics), positive body motions (kinesics) and body language, and positive touch (haptics) when appropriate.
- Cover personal values.
- Maintain a positive, neutral stance.
- Use positive power and positive control.
- Control personal anger—avoid antagonizing or harassing interviewees.
- Don't use coercive behavior.
- Use observation, evaluation, and assessment.
- Avoid the third degree (mental or physical torture used in an effort to gain a confession).
- Use closed questions and open questions when appropriate.
- Keep questions simple, and avoid ambiguously worded questions.
- Dare to ask tough questions.
- Mentally assume an affirmative answer.
- Use leading questions appropriately, and ask self-appraisal questions.
- Handle trial balloons calmly.
- Assume more information is available.

First Impressions

You make your first impression during the first 10 to 45 seconds of an interview. This is your opportunity to show that you are calm, cool, collected, friendly, firm, fair, human, and compassionate. First impressions are important in helping to cement a close, but temporary, relationship to encourage the interviewee's cooperation. In those first seconds of human interaction, you convey your intentions through nonverbal messages. You express human warmth through your tone of voice and your gestures and mannerisms. These things significantly affect the outcome of the interview.

Although face-to-face interviews are preferred, telephone interviews are sometimes necessary. In a telephone interview, you can express your positive qualities through your tone of voice, timing, and silences. On occasion, an interviewee will confess or make some significant admission within the first few minutes of the interview without being specifically encouraged to do so. Be ready for this.

The Interviewee's Evaluation Process

Observation, evaluation, assessment, and intuition are vital elements of investigative problem solving. They usually begin with the first verbal and nonverbal exchanges in an encounter, and they continue until the end. You can expect the interviewee to start an evaluation process with his or her first glimpse of you. How do you look? Do you appear to be a professional? How do you sound? Do you sound overbearing? Ruthless? Warm and caring? Consciously or subconsciously, even the slowest, least educated interviewees evaluate you to decide whether it is safe to reveal information or whether they will be abused in the process. The interviewee evaluation process takes place whether you want it to or not. Remember that your tone of voice, choice of words, and body language express particular attitudes. This is the time to signal that you want the interview to be a friendly interaction.

Subsequent interviewees will evaluate the interview process, in part, based on how you treated preceding interviewees. The message about you and your methods will be conveyed to everyone—that you are okay or not, fair or not, biased or not. There is no question that you will be judged.

There is some strategic advantage if the interviewee is not under arrest when interviewed; faced with less of a threat, the interviewee experiences less distress and is more likely to cooperate. Although the interviewee may still be uncomfortable, your professional demeanor and friendly ways will make you seem worthy of receiving important information.

Elements of Contact

Introduction and Greeting   A formal introduction will help establish you as someone in whom it is safe to confide. When possible, it is useful to separate yourself from any prior investigations of the crime you are asked to solve. For example, I speak softly, not in a weak fashion but in a modulated tone that I hope will convey my confidence and human warmth. I might say, "Hello, I'm Mr. Yeschke. Would you follow me, please?" as I meet the interviewee in a waiting room before we walk to my office down the hall. Then, when we reach my office, I may say, "Please, have a seat here," as I motion to a particular chair.

During the first few minutes, the tone of the interview is determined, and it may last for minutes, hours, or days. If an interviewee offers to shake hands when we meet, then I do, but I don't routinely offer a handshake to each interviewee. I usually try to maintain a professional aloofness to signal the serious nature of the inquiry. I try to appear reserved, not stuffy. Generally, I feel that small talk is not appropriate, and I avoid all forms of intimidation and abusiveness that might in any way spark resentment or defensiveness. I want victims, witnesses, and suspects alike to feel free to talk to me.

Greeting interviewees cordially helps them feel at ease. Despite your innocent manner, try your best to encourage them to provide the information you need. Help interviewees to relax enough that they do not feel threatened, but bear in mind that eliminating all tension is neither possible nor to your advantage. Some degree of tension in an interview often helps the interviewee think actively and respond productively (OSS Assessment Office 1948, p. 138).

Seating   For the interview, choose a location that provides both privacy and comfort. Determine the seating arrangements in advance. When possible, I arrange the chairs so that the interviewee and I will face one another across a space of six to eight feet and there will be an uncluttered wall behind me. As the interview progresses, I usually move my chair to within about four feet of the interviewee. I try to use chairs of similar design and comfort. Obviously, chairs and their location are a ridiculous consideration at an accident scene, but the important point is to avoid moving too fast into the interviewee's personal space.

Announcing Your Objective   Announce the objective of the interview in answer to the interviewee's usually unasked question about why he or she is being interviewed. Tell the interviewee that you want to determine how the incident you're investigating happened and that you want to prevent similar events from occurring in the future. For example, you might say, "The purpose of our talk today is to discuss the building materials that are missing from the warehouse. I'm looking for information that will help me determine how the materials were removed so that I can make clear recommendations to prevent another disappearance in the future. I'm interviewing several people, and I need your assistance to get a better view of the circumstances. First, let me get a little background data about you to get to know you a little better." By orienting interviewees to the objective of your interview, you encourage them to be less secretive and defensive. When they realize the seriousness of your inquiry, interviewees may comply more completely. Never announce your objective as identifying and prosecuting the guilty party. Although interviewees often want to know how their interview is relevant and significant to your inquiry, it is not wise to explain your overall objectives or hypothesis (Dexter 1970, p. 32). Too much explanation may cause them to become apprehensive about how their help might harm fellow human beings, reducing their willingness to cooperate. Alternatively, they might not accept your explanation and might provide only limited data that might not be truthful (Bennis et al. 1973, p. 216). Hence, too much explanation gives directive powers, the power to lead an interview down a particular path, to interviewees unnecessarily.

When beginning an interview, adopt an open manner that invites the interviewee to share any thoughts, observations, opinions, or facts that have any bearing on the crime. This invitation should be implied, not actually spoken, and you should show appreciation for the cooperation when it comes. If there is a time to open the door to the truth, it is at this point of the discussion, in the first four minutes, when the interviewee is determining whether it is okay to talk to you. In those first minutes, the interviewee senses if you are neutral or biased, if you are trying to gather facts or taking unfair advantage of people.

Setting the Tone   After you have announced the objective and during those critical first few minutes of the interaction, ask the interviewee questions that will be easy to answer: the spelling of his or her name, date of birth, number of years of employment, current position, years of education, marital status. These questions give the interviewee the opportunity to vent some emotional energy and to feel more comfortable. At this stage of the investigation, you may note evasiveness and lack of cooperation. From the beginning, use positive tactics that encourage cooperation, such as active listening, empathy, respect, and believability.

Forensic interviews are not intense interactions in which verbal combat takes place. Try for a soft harmony to promote comfort and thought. Use a toned-down style to avoid any suggestion of intense confrontation. When discussing the circumstances of the incident, I recommend that you use the word *if* to soften the questioning. Using *if* tends to prevent any implied accusation in your voice. Too often, investigators interrogate every interviewee in a prosecutorial manner in hopes of quickly unmasking the guilty party. I see no justification for treating every interviewee as though he or she were guilty. I avoid using quick questions and burning stares. At the outset of each interview, my choice of words and phrases is intended to exhibit my positive attitude and expectations. Setting a positive tone with each interviewee pays off. Doing so communicates a professional self-image.

Contact at the Crime Scene

At a crime scene, the victim's fear is so immediate and powerful that it cannot be dissipated by the victim's exercise of self-control alone. Your patience and assistance will be required. A hurried approach will only cause confusion and heighten the victim's distress. Calm the victim by saying something like "You're safe now." Showing proper regard for the victim's feelings builds empathy, which facilitates questioning and promotes accurate recollections. Fear of reprisal and intimidation may prevent witnesses as well as victims from cooperating; to prevent intimidation, move witnesses away from suspects before identifying and interviewing them. Ask witnesses to recall everything observed during the incident; be sure that you don't contaminate the information they provide. For example, as the witness presents recall, avoid editorializing by interpreting as the recall progresses, otherwise you may find the recall tends to follow your expectation or interpretation. Therefore, keep your evaluation to yourself so as not to influence the recall.

Because of the urgency of some criminal investigations, it is not always possible to prepare fully for an interview. In such a situation, gather basic information immediately; later, in a recontact interview, obtain additional facts under more favorable conditions. Remember, though, that the greater the time lapse between the incident and the interview, the less likely it is that witnesses will be able to report accurately what they observed. In addition, they may be reluctant to cooperate fully once the excitement of the situation has subsided. Contamination is another concern. People tend to seek group consensus, and they will often adopt the group opinion as their own regardless of whether they believe it to be correct. If not separated quickly and interviewed, witnesses may compare stories and may adopt parts of the accounts of others at the crime scene. Make a special point of interviewing alibi witnesses promptly to reduce the possibility that suspect and witness will take the opportunity to corroborate their stories and cover up the suspect's participation in the crime.

PRIMARY PHASE

The primary phase follows the contact section of the initial phase of the interview. During the primary phase, the interviewer strengthens the rapport begun in the contact section, gathers more information through active listening, and watches for signs of deception. By this point, you have established that you are open to discussion, and when you are seen as a warm person, you are more likely to gain the information you are seeking.

At the beginning of the primary phase (Figure 9.6), the interviewer gradually moves his or her chair closer to the interviewee (the moderate location discussed in Chapter 10). Between points B and C of the interview process (Figure 9.7), the investigator reviews the case information with the interviewee as a prelude to asking additional questions. All the while, he or she tries to maintain a positive tone and build rapport.

Exactly how you will proceed—which questions you will ask and how you will formulate them—depends as much on the quality of the interaction you have been able to establish as on the facts you need to gather. The investigator's adaptability is vital. Being able to think on your feet is important to seeking out the truth. (See Chapter 11 for more on question formulation.) The investigator moves from a structured to a semistructured approach between points C and D on the polyphasic flowchart (see Figure 9.1). Encourage interviewees to think carefully and to try to remember details. Allow them the time they need to think. Don't interrogate yet! That will come later.

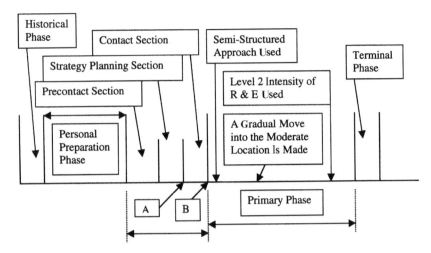

Figure 9.6   The primary phase. During this part of the interview, the investigator observes, evaluates, and assesses the interviewee's verbal and nonverbal behavior.

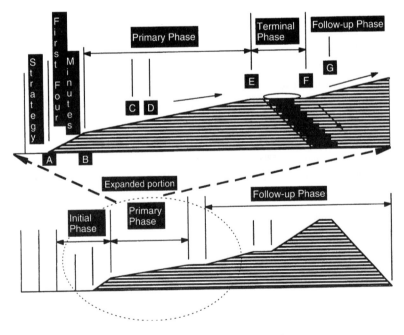

Figure 9.7   Expanded view showing the primary phase.

"Bones"

Around points C and D on the flowchart, I begin to use what I call *bones*—nonaccusatory questions that reveal the elements of the complete incident. These semistructured questions work together, much as the bones of the body make up a whole skeleton. In the same way that muscle and tissue surround our bones, all of the details of the incident and the interviewee's involvement surround the central facts of the incident. The semistructured questions you use in this phase of the interview are designed to reveal, through an interviewee's pattern of responses, whether he or she is lying or telling the truth.

Move with compassion, and continue to use the hidden persuaders throughout the primary phase. Without being obvious, try to imply that you are seeking the interviewee's permission to ask the questions as you proceed. Avoid hasty conclusions and accusations. Don't abruptly stop interviewing and begin trying to gain an admission or confession. Remember that culpable individuals hesitate to reveal a truth that brings shame, embarrassment, and possible punishment. As a lead-in to using the bones, you might say, "As I mentioned before, I'm trying to determine how the loss occurred. So, let me ask you a few questions." Then proceed with the following series of questions, remembering to remain flexible and keeping in mind the value of the floating-point strategy.

The Narration Question

At some logical point during the primary phase, ask the interviewee to tell you what happened—what he or she knows of the incident under investigation. Truthful interviewees tend to provide smooth-flowing narratives that have been clearly thought out. They may offer suggestions to help you solve the matter. Untruthful interviewees will weigh everything they say, causing awkward pauses in their narration. Once the narrative is complete, review and summarize details to ensure that the report is complete. Allow the interviewee unrestricted recall, then ask specific questions to uncover details. All the while, take notes to show that you are attentive.

The "You" Question

Address the interviewee by name, and begin this question by saying, "It's important to get this matter cleared up." Briefly review the reported incident, and explain that you are asking these questions in an effort to determine what happened. The "You" question might take several forms. Here are a few examples:

> "If you're the one who did it, it's important to get it cleared up. How do you stand on this? Did you steal the traveler's checks?"
> "The report claims that you spoke with Rita just before the fire broke out. If you did, it's important to get this straightened out and clear things up. Jim, let me ask, did you have any contact with Rita just before the fire broke out?"

An interviewee who has a high level of shame and remorse and cannot stand the stress of the investigation may provide a full confession at this point. This is a rare occurrence, however. Do not ask the "You" question accusingly, and do nothing to suggest that the interviewee is responsible for the incident or is lying. Instead, adopt a positive tone of open curiosity. "If the interviewee is hiding something, your genuine curiosity will provoke unease and evasion exhibited by such outward signs as squirming and preening. Such signs of evasion and possible deception may take place in about a hundredth of a second. You should be attentive and notice these signals without being obvious (Yeschke 1993, p. 93).

The "Who" Question

You might begin the "Who" question with a preamble, such as, "Knowing for sure who did set the fire in the warehouse is one thing, but having suspicions is something else. Do you know for sure who set the fire?" The interviewee will probably answer negatively, which leads easily into the next question.

The "Suspicion" Question

Then you might say, "Okay, you don't know for sure who did it. But let me ask: Do you have any suspicions of who might have set the fire?" Quickly add the caveat, "Keep in mind that I'm not asking you to be malicious, to arbitrarily point a finger at anyone or anything like that, because that wouldn't be fair. I'm just wondering if anyone has done anything or said anything to cause you to think they might have set the fire. Can you think of anyone who might have been involved?" Typical responses from nonculpable interviewees include these: "I can't imagine who did it or why." "I can't believe it even happened here." "If one of my coworkers did it, he would have to be a Jekyll-and-Hyde personality."

The "Trust" Question

This question usually takes the form, "Who comes to mind that you trust? Who, do you think, could not possibly have stolen the computer equipment?" or "Of all the people who had the opportunity, who, do you think, would not have taken the money?"

The "Verification" Question

"After considering the situation, do you think the money was really stolen, or do you think the theft report is false?" The culpable may say they don't think the loss was caused by theft. "It must have been a mistake or misplaced in some way." The blameless tend to acknowledge the report as correct, saying the theft was real.

The "Approach" Question

"Life presents many temptations for all of us. Let me ask you this: Have any of the truckers ever asked you to divert a cargo?" The blameless interviewee acknowledges that there was some discussion but never took it seriously enough to mention. The culpable ones latch on to such discussions as an opportunity to cast blame on others and report that discussions took place.

The "Thoughts" Question

"There are so many demands and pressures on people in their daily lives that they occasionally fantasize about doing things. Now, as far as you're concerned, do you recall ever thinking of having sex with Mary Sue even though you never actually did?" To report a fantasy of having sex with Mary Sue tell me that the culpable interviewee considers the thinking meaningful, memorable enough to recall. "Well, there have been times when she rubs herself against me and I think she really wants me to touch her sexually." The innocent do not consider such fleeting moments significant and deny involvement.

The "Instruction" Question

This question is useful when investigating charges of child sexual abuse. "Many people teach their kids about sex as they're growing up. After all, it's the responsibility of the parent to teach their children about things like health. You certainly don't want anyone taking advantage of them. What comes to mind about telling your kids things about sex?"

The "Willingness" Question

"If the investigation shows that you actually did leave the store with groceries you didn't pay for, would you be willing to explain it and get this matter straightened out? Would you be willing to pay for those missing things?"

The "Consequences" Questions

The next few questions ask the interviewee about the consequences for certain actions. For example, you might ask, "Let's assume that we find out the report was not true. What should happen to Jane for her false accusation?" Then, give time for the response and do not rush to ask the second question: "If we find out who took Jane's purse, what should happen to that person?" The culpable will want to give the thief a break, while the nonculpable will want to see the culpable caught.

If the interviewee does not suggest jail for the guilty party, ask, "How about jail for that person?" Innocent interviewees usually respond, "I should think so! That pervert!" or something to that effect. They answer smoothly, giving their judgment without hesitation. The deceptive, on the other hand, tend to be lenient toward the guilty party or evasive in their responses. They might say, for example, "Well, jail seems a little harsh," or "It really depends on the circumstances. Maybe the person was under a lot of stress." Stress, then later, could be the basis of an interrogative approach.

The "Kind to Do It" Question

Your next question might be, "What kind of person do you think would do something like this?" Nonculpable people quickly provide an appropriate response, such as, "Some sick person!" or "Someone who doesn't care about making us go through this." The deceptive will tend to rationalize or evade the question, responding, "Someone who is under a lot of pressure!" or "I'm not that kind of person! I'm not a pervert!"

The "Why It Happened" Question

Then you might ask, "Why do you think a person would do this sort of thing?" You might expect the nonculpable to respond quickly and clearly, "I have no idea," whereas the culpable might respond, "No reason!" or "There's a divorce case!" or "The people here aren't paid enough!" The culpable often try to give the thief an excuse or rationalization.

The "They Say You Did It" Question

When you ask, "Is there any reason for anyone to say you broke into the storeroom?" innocent interviewees might respond, "No, I don't think so. I didn't do it." They will appear to consider whether they could have given anyone a reason to suspect them. Rather than squirm and look guilty, they may furrow their brow, squint, or look contemplative. This body language is fleeting and difficult to fake convincingly.

The "They Say They Saw You" Question

Follow up the preceding question with, "Is there any reason that anyone might say they saw you breaking into the storeroom?" The innocent might say, "No, because I didn't do it!" They will respond quickly and without contemplation because they don't need deep thought to know what they did. The culpable party might say, "Well, let me see. . . . Uh, no, I don't think so."

The "What Would You Say" Question

This question asks the interviewee to think about the person responsible for the incident. Ask something like this: "Let's assume the ring was actually stolen. If the guilty person were here standing before you, what would you say to him or her?" Interviewees with nothing to hide often respond, "What you did was wrong!" or "That was a stupid thing to do!" The response will come quickly and smoothly, often as an angry blast of indignation and condemnation. Deceptive interviewees will often be hard-pressed to find words of condemnation.

The "Expanding Inquiry" Question

"Do you mind having the investigation extend beyond your family to your neighbors and coworkers?" The culpable may hesitate to have an inquiry go out of the immediate work area. If it is brought to the attention of friends and neighbors, someone may comment on what seemed like suspicious behavior, such as a recent vacation or large purchase. The nonculpable ones don't mind the extended inquiry because they generally don't have anything to hide.

THE TERMINAL PHASE

Between points E and F of the polyphasic flowchart (see Figure 9.1) lies the terminal phase, a turning point in the interview. During this phase, the investigator draws a conclusion about the interviewee's veracity. He or she synthesizes all of the interviewee's verbal and nonverbal responses into a significant pattern indicating one of the following:

- Truthfulness
- Probable truthfulness
- Possible truthfulness
- Possible deception
- Probable deception
- Deception

The first step in the terminal phase is to determine whether the interviewee has answered your questions fully and truthfully. The second step involves planning what to do next.

Step 1

By the beginning of the terminal phase, you will have had the opportunity to observe, evaluate, and assess the interviewee, noting how the pattern of his or her responses compares to the totality of the evidence. You will have had enough time to become confident in your conclusion. Generally, one interview will offer sufficient indicators to guide your conclusions, but not always. There are certainly no absolutes in such assessments, but I'm convinced that nonverbal signals are meaningful indicators of deception. I think it's fair to say, based on my experience, that certain behavior signals characterize deceptive individuals while other behavior signals characterize the truthful. When interviewees are inconsistent or deceptive, it is as though they are trying to force a blue puzzle piece into a space intended for a brown piece. Differences become evident when the investigator considers the totality of the circumstances.

Even cooperative interviewees might show some indications of holding back information. Victims may hide some of the details of an incident because they are embarrassed over their victimization. Witnesses may appear to be holding back information because they feel self-conscious about not having done more to aid the victim or stop the thief. On the other hand, inconsistencies in a victim's or witness's story may indicate that he or she fabricated the crime. Perhaps the interviewee actually stole the money herself or arranged for a buddy to steal it in a mock holdup. A witness who was a co-conspirator in the crime has good reason to feel uneasy over being questioned about the details of the incident. And of course, the perpetrator will try to hold back information. Criminals with little practice tend to stumble over routine investigative questions, showing telltale signs of involvement.

For a variety of reasons, investigators sometimes enter the terminal phase of an interview without having reached a conclusion about the interviewee's truthfulness. If this occurs, you might try one of the following:

- Comment that it looks as if the interviewee has more information to provide.
- Tell the interviewee that a second interview will be set up in the near future to review a few things.
- Give the impression that you suspect that the interviewee is hiding or holding back important information.

Step 2

By the end of the terminal phase, after using both the structured and semistructured approaches, evaluate whether there is a need for further interviewing using the nonstructured approach or whether it would be appropriate to seek an admission or a confession through interrogation.

If this is to be the end of the interview, leave your business card and ask the interviewee to contact you if he or she remembers anything new. If there are inconsistencies that you wish to clarify, you might decide to continue the interview or to schedule another. To verify information that the interviewee has supplied, you might try to schedule a detection-of-deception examination. No matter what course you choose, maintain rapport. This is not a time to put on the nasty-guy hat.

THE FOLLOW-UP PHASE

The last phase of the interview process is the follow-up phase, which occurs between points F and M on the polyphasic flowchart (see Figure 9.1). During this final phase of the interview process, inconsistencies are resolved, confrontation may take place, and confessions may be obtained. At this point, you have considerable flexibility in applying the floating-point strategy. Maintain rapport, continue to listen actively, and avoid radical direction (changes of a sweeping or extreme nature) or any use of abuse, coercion, harassment, or intimidation.

Between flowchart points F and G, you might decide to review the interviewee's responses, point out inconsistencies, and hint at the interviewee's deception. Seek the truth using increased review and encouragement at this turning point. Proceed cautiously. A premature announcement of your suspicions may only encourage the interviewee to do a better job of covering the truth.

Step 3

Depending on the circumstances of the investigation, you may decide to pursue one of the following courses:

- Arrange for the interviewee to take a detection-of-deception examination.

- Schedule a new interview with the interviewee, allowing yourself time to prepare for a second interview and possible interrogation.
- Begin an attempt to gain an admission or confession from the subject.

Once interviewees claim that the information they are providing is truthful, you can ask if they would be willing to undergo a detection-of-deception (polygraph) examination. This suggestion might be made at several places during the process: between points G and H, between points H and I, or about point L on the flowchart. The timing depends on the situation and on how the suggestion fits into the overall process. Some people will not agree to undergo a polygraph examination no matter how helpful you tell them it will be. Others will be reluctant but will eventually submit to it.

There are two important things to consider before requesting an interviewee to undergo a polygraph examination. First, it is important to be convinced that the polygraph is a practical, functional, and trustworthy investigative tool. Second, you should ensure that the forensic psychophysiologist chosen to administer the examination will provide high-quality, professional service. Although polygraph examinations are not 100 percent accurate, they have proved to be highly reliable (Yeschke 1993).

Step 4

After attempting to resolve inconsistencies in the interviewee's story between points F and H, you may decide to take further action. If you are convinced that the interviewee is involved, directly or indirectly, in the matter under investigation, you will reveal this between points H and I. If you are ready to point out inconsistencies in the interviewee's story, the next thing to do is to announce your conclusion to the interviewee. To begin the interrogation, you might confront the subject by saying, for example,

- "It looks as if you haven't told me the whole truth."
- "It seems to me that you are holding something back."

- "I'm uneasy about what you've told me here today. I believe you've got more to tell me."
- "I think you're the one who did it, and it's important for us to talk about this to get it cleared up."

Use care when making such statements. You don't want to frighten the subject. For an investigator to express such a conclusion takes some daring and skill. Although there is no need to harshly accuse or intimidate the interviewee, this is the time for specific review and persistent encouragement to clear up inconsistencies or to gain an admission or a confession. It is at this point that the interview gradually flows into an interrogation. The interviewer-turned-interrogator now clearly and specifically announces that the subject seems to be intentionally withholding information and is probably a key player in the matter under investigation. While you announce your suspicions, you should continue to help the subject save face and rationalize his or her involvement. This is no time to degrade or humiliate the subject. Coercion has no place here—or indeed anywhere in this process.

Up to this time, you have modified your efforts to deal with embarrassed victims and reluctant witnesses, but now is the time to forge ahead into an interrogation to seek an admission or a confession. Don't be destructive in your efforts. Don't label the interrogatee when addressing him or her. In other words, don't say, "I know you're the molester." Not only are such comments hostile, but they are self-defeating.

Be certain, and be confident! This is no longer the time for using the word *if*. Instead, display confidence in the subject's involvement. Interrogation is not for all investigators. It is a matter of temperament, confidence, and skill. Some investigators are more capable than others of handling this concentrated search for the truth.

Your efforts may yield only an incomplete admission of guilt. If you doubt that the subject told the complete story of what happened, remember that even a partial confession can be helpful in concluding the investigation. That is not to say that you should be satisfied with a half-done job. Accept whatever confession or admission is offered, and have it witnessed and put into written form. Then commit yourself to starting over with renewed effort to seek more details of the subject's culpability.

REVIEW QUESTIONS

1. How and when do we learn bias and prejudice?

2. How can we change our attitudes as we mature?

3. Name the three sections of the initial phase, and describe the interviewer's task in each.

4. What is the floating-point strategy, and how can you use it during an investigation?

5. Where can you find hints of motivation?

6. How can you evaluate potential interviewees, and why should you do this?

7. What should you consider when planning an interview strategy?

8. What does it mean to have an open mind as an interviewer?

9. What is the main purpose of the first four minutes of an interview?

10. What are hidden persuaders, and how can you use them in an interview?

11. Which of the hidden persuaders do you think are most effective?

12. How can you make a positive impression in the first few seconds of an interview?

13. How does the interviewee evaluate the investigator? What is he or she trying to determine?

14. What is the strategic advantage in interviewing someone who is not under arrest?

15. What are the elements of the contact section?

16. What should you tell the interviewee about the objective of the interview?

17. How can you put the interviewee at ease to promote cooperation?

18. What tactics can you use when interviewing victims and witnesses at a crime scene?

19. What is the interviewer's task in the primary phase?

20. What are "bones," and what do they help the interviewer determine?

21. Why is it useful to have the interviewee provide a narrative of what happened?

22. What is the interviewer's task in the terminal phase?

23. What occurs during the follow-up phase?

24. What might you say to the subject as you flow from interviewing into interrogating?

10

Setting, Location, Intensity, and Approach in the Interview

To ensure the success of an interview, the investigator must consider many factors, including where the interview will take place, how the participants will be positioned within the interview room, how intensely the interviewer will press for information, and what approach he or she will use in questioning the interviewee. All of these elements require careful planning because they have a significant impact on the outcome of every interview. This chapter suggests ways in which environmental setting, participant location, intensity, and approach can be incorporated into the interview process.

ENVIRONMENTAL SETTING

Privacy is a key element of successful interviews. When possible, arrange to conduct your interviews in a comfortable, private room. The environment you choose should be quiet and free from disturbances. However, there is little to gain by transporting interviewees to some distant site that you think is ideal. Doing so might cause unnecessary disruption. Virtually any site that provides privacy will probably be suitable.

LOCATION OF PARTICIPANTS

Personal Space

There is an invisible boundary, known as *personal space,* around each of us. We become uncomfortable when strangers intrude in our personal space. Most Americans reserve about a foot and a half of space around them for intimate conversation. They allow casual interactions in the space between about a foot and a half to about four feet. Impersonal transactions take place beyond about four feet. Personal space varies not only with culture (Hall 1966), but also with social status. People of high status assume and are granted more personal space than people of lower status.

Proxemics is the study of the spatial distances that people maintain between themselves and others. A knowledge of proxemics can help you become a better interviewer. Recognize that there is an invisible boundary—a protective wall of privacy—around interviewees (Bennis et al. 1973, p. 78). Whether standing or sitting during an interview, be sensitive to the interviewee's level of comfort, and use it to determine how the interviewee defines his or her personal space. Enter this space with care to avoid alarming the interviewee. Moving too quickly into the interviewee's personal space may cause undue stress, which could block the flow of communication. This action is unnecessary and self-defeating (Davis 1975, p. 180).

Conversation, Moderate, and Intimate Locations

I believe that it is helpful to identify three distinct distances between interview participants. In order of decreasing physical distance, I call these the *conversation, moderate,* and *intimate locations.* When I say "location," I mean to include both distance and position. Most interviews take place in the conversation or moderate location.

As you begin the interview, position yourself in the conversation location, about six feet away from the interviewee, and then gradually move closer into the moderate location, where you can conduct most of the interview. Not only does moving closer convey your warmth, but also it will help both you and the interviewee focus more fully on the discussion. The display of positive motives generally sparks productive results. The intimate locations are used when the interviewee needs comforting, when using intensity level 4 (see below), or during other portions of the follow-up phase. Of course, space limitations may prevent you from beginning the interview in the conversation location or moving closer to the interviewee than the moderate location.

The Conversation Location

In the conversation location, the interview participants are situated about six feet apart, as shown in Figures 10.1 and 10.2. This is a "safe" distance for the interviewee, just beyond easy physical reach. In this location, participants have enough room to lean forward without touching and can move their legs comfortably. The conversation location permits the investigator to observe the interviewee for nonverbal communication at critical moments. The conversation location is used between points A and C of the polyphasic flowchart shown in Chapter 9 (see Figure 9.1).

At the beginning of the interview, position your chair to the left or right of the interviewee's chair at an angle of about 45 degrees. Avoid facing the interviewee squarely and presenting yourself symbolically as a threat. It is preferable that there be no obstruction between participants other than the corner of a desk. You can lean back or forward in your chair, depending on the context of the interview. However, avoid leaning your chair back against a wall, and don't put your feet up on the desk. Keep your

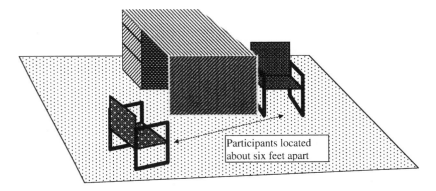

Figure 10.1 The conversation location. The interview participants are located about six feet apart.

body position alert, and project an attentive, professional appearance at all times.

Begin the interview with yourself and the interviewee in the conversation location. Be careful not to violate the interviewee's personal space. If you go past that invisible line and step into the interviewee's "flight area," he or she will probably back off to increase the space between you. The interviewee's flight area is located somewhere within the moderate location.

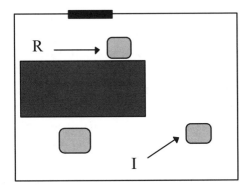

Figure 10.2 Overhead view of a typical interview room, ten by twelve feet, showing participants in the conversation location. I = interviewer; R = respondent.

The Moderate Location

The moderate location brings interview participants to within about four feet of one another, as shown in Figures 10.3 and 10.4. This is close enough to allow the investigator to gently touch the interviewee's arm or shoulder if appropriate. In the moderate location, participants are generally situated at a 45-degree angle, as in the conversation location. At this distance, legs can be

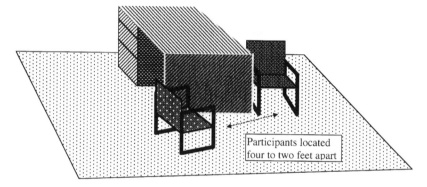

Participants located
four to two feet apart

Figure 10.3   The moderate location. The investigator gradually and inconspicuously moves closer to the interviewee until they are about four feet apart.

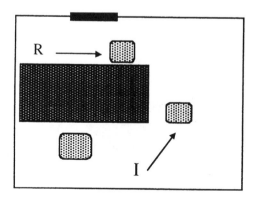

Figure 10.4   Overhead view of a typical interview room, ten by twelve feet, showing participants in the moderate location. I = interviewer; R = respondent.

crossed carefully. Most interviews and many interrogations can be conducted from the moderate location.

The Intimate Locations

In the first intimate location, the participants are situated about two feet apart, as shown in Figures 10.5 and 10.6. As the intensity of the interview increases, the interviewer moves into the second intimate location, to within about a foot of the interviewee and facing him or her, as shown in Figures 10.7 and 10.8. The intimate locations may be the most stressful or the most reassuring, depending on how the interview is conducted. In these locations, you can easily reach the interviewee. Your chair is situated quite close to the interviewee's chair, so that your knee is next to the interviewee's knee. In this position, the crossing of legs is next to impossible. This distance is reserved for in-depth interviews requiring intense interpersonal communication, great empathy, and lots of encouragement. It is also used for interrogations in which an admission or a confession is sought.

The investigator's shift in position from intimate location 1 to intimate location 2 often accompanies a change in the interview strategy, from resolving inconsistencies (interviewing) to attempting to gain an admission or a confession (interrogating). The suc-

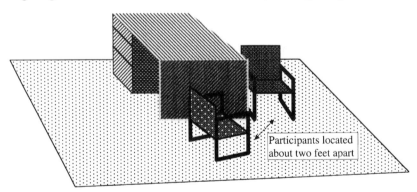

Participants located about two feet apart

Figure 10.5 The first intimate location. Participants are seated about two feet apart.

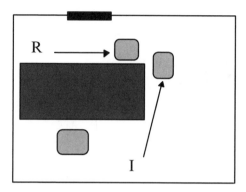

Figure 10.6   Overhead view of a typical interview room, ten by twelve feet, showing participants in the first intimate location. I = interviewer; R = respondent.

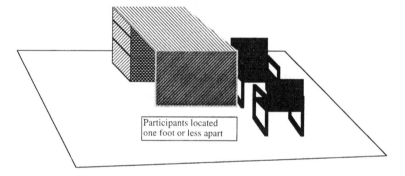

Participants located one foot or less apart

Figure 10.7   The second intimate location. Participants are seated about one foot apart.

cessful investigator will make this transition smoothly, not only in shifting position, but also in the comments, questions, and intensity he or she employs. In the intimate locations, the rhetorical questions and statements used differ from the investigator's previous efforts to assist the interviewee to rationalize and save face.

REVIEW AND ENCOURAGEMENT INTENSITIES

Throughout the interview, the investigator reviews the facts of the case and their implications with the interviewee and encourages

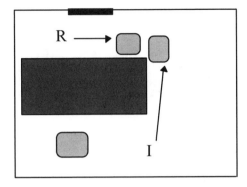

Figure 10.8   Overhead view of a typical interview room, ten feet by twelve feet, showing participants in the second intimate location. I = interviewer; R = respondent.

him or her to answer questions truthfully. Using verbal and non-verbal communication, the investigator tries to persuade the interviewee to reveal information or to make an admission or a confession. The intensity of this review and encouragement varies throughout the different stages of the interview process. The objective of using varying degrees of intensity is to bring out verbal and nonverbal signals that indicate that the interviewee is lying. Intensity, the amount of effort put into how remarkable or powerful the investigator's presentation is, is signaled by the investigator's total presentation: how and where the participants are seated; the investigator's tone of voice, facial expressions, and body language; and the investigator's questions and comments and how they are formulated.

Review

The topics the investigator chooses to review with the interviewee vary with the phases of the interview, as does the intensity of that review. From general to more specific, the investigator's level of review might increase as follows:

- Inquiry into the circumstances of the matter under investigation.

- Discussion regarding the interviewee's knowledge, opportunity, access, and motivation as they relate to the matter under investigation.
- Coverage of the totality of the circumstances as related to the interviewee's knowledge, opportunity, access, and motivation.
- Consideration of the totality of the circumstances in lesser or greater depth.
- Consideration of the interviewee's relationship to the totality of the circumstances with less or more focus.

Encouragement

The reason to encourage the interviewee is to reassure him or her and to reach a certain objective—the truth. During the process of trying to reach that goal, only positive methods to encourage the interviewee to tell the truth are suggested:

- Persuading
- Selling
- Influencing
- Calling for the truth

The use of review and encouragement does not involve bullying, threatening, coercing, or punishing the interviewee.

Intensity Levels

Now let's look at each intensity level and illustrate the specific kinds of review and encouragement that operate at each level.

Level 1

Level 1, representing general review and minimal encouragement, is used in all interviews from point A to between points C and D on the polyphasic flowchart (see Figure 9.1). At this level, the least amount of effort is employed in using review and encouragement. No attempt is made to point out gaps or inconsistencies in the interviewee's story. Level 1 is also used for the preliminary inquiry during the precontact section of the initial phase. While obtaining details regarding the matter under investigation, it isn't appropriate to challenge the information provided. There will be a time for that later, if necessary.

Level 2

Level 2, used from between points C and D to point F on the flowchart, represents the greatest amount of general review and minimal encouragement. Compared to level 1, there is more effort in this level to use these tools. No gaps in the interviewee's story are pointed out or challenged, but some effort is made to clarify details. The "bones" discussed in Chapter 9 are used to draw out the truth. At this intensity level, interviewees may, through verbal and nonverbal signs, indicate that they are trying to dodge your questions or are providing dishonest answers.

Level 3

Used between points F and I of the flowchart, intensity level 3 involves specific review and persistent encouragement. At this level, the interviewer discusses any inconsistencies that he or she noted earlier in the interview. This is not a time to interrogate, but rather a time to revisit investigative detail. The interviewer must be bold enough to state clearly that there are inconsistencies that must be resolved. The investigator tries to persuade the interviewee that it is inevitable that the truth will eventually be discovered.

During this level, culpable interviewees will probably reveal further signs of their deception. Then it is time for the interviewer to take on the role of interrogator and look for an admission or a confession. The interviewer puts on a different hat, so to speak, becoming assertive and more determined. Between points H and I of the interview process, the interrogator begins to sell the subject on the idea of telling the truth to "get this thing cleared up." Having taken this road, the interrogator cannot back down—unless he or she becomes convinced that it's the wrong direction.

Don't rush to use intensity level 3 with interviewees as soon as you notice inconsistencies. Make it a general rule to tune in to inconsistencies during the primary phase without pouncing on interviewees because of them. Throughout the interview, gradually focus attention on the inconsistencies and become more assertive in pointing out gaps in the interviewee's story. Become less accepting of excuses while you begin to challenge the patterns of deception. Sell the interviewee on the idea of willingly divulging the truth.

Level 4

This level, used between points I and K on the flowchart, represents a greater intensity of specific review and persistent encouragement than level 3. Sometimes even the victim is found to be lying and is then interrogated. Most interviewees never reach this level of interaction, however, because the investigator decides that they are being truthful. Remember that it is a mistake to interrogate everyone as though they were guilty or deceptive. Level 4 reaches its greatest intensity between points J and K as the interrogator attempts to gain an admission or a confession. (A confession includes several significant incriminatory statements, whereas an admission is one or more incriminatory statements of a more minor nature.) This level of intensity includes greater efforts to help the subject rationalize and save face while he or she confesses total or partial responsibility for the matter under investigation.

Level 5

Level 5 is used between points K and M on the flowchart. It represents about the same intensity of specific review and persistent encouragement as in level 4, however, level 5 represents more effort by the investigator in reviewing and encouraging more focus of energy and determination. The interrogator moves closer to the subject while showing a greater degree of certainty that the subject committed the crime. More persuasion is used in level 5 to sell the subject on the idea to confess. By this point in the interrogation, the interrogatee may have provided an admission but not a complete confession. At point L, the investigator decides whether to ask the subject to undergo a detection-of-deception examination to confirm the supposedly limited nature of his or her involvement.

APPROACHES

The interview process outlined in this book involves three approaches built around the kinds of questions asked. These three approaches—the structured, semistructured, and nonstructured approaches—are illustrated in the polyphasic flowchart in Chapter 9 (see Figure 9.1).

The Structured Approach

The structured approach is used at the beginning of the interview and forms the baseline for the investigator's direct observation, evaluation, and assessment of the interviewee. This approach begins at point A of the flowchart and ends between points C and D. In this portion of the interview, the investigator asks basic fact-finding questions without accusation or intimidation. These questions require less deep thought from the interviewee than those asked during the semistructured and nonstructured modes. To encourage the interviewee to respond, ask questions that he or she can answer easily. I use routine questions for this purpose, such as the spelling of the interviewee's name, the number of years of schooling, and the type of work done in the past.

The questions asked in the structured approach are not directly related to solving the investigative problem. Instead, they give the interviewee an opportunity to evaluate the investigator and to determine whether he or she will be treated fairly. Everything the investigator does sends a signal to the interviewee. Every part of the investigator's presentation encourages or discourages cooperation. Certainly, if the interviewee is hostile by nature to everyone in authority or is determined to lie, little of what you do and say during the interview will make any difference. Often, however, you can nudge reluctant interviewees into a more compliant stance and eventually even nurture the guilty party into a position to admit or confess.

At first, you can expect some delay in the interviewee's responses. Do not automatically consider this to be a significant indication of potential deception. Note how clearly the interviewee answers the question; this will help you determine the interviewee's ability to handle more complex questions later in the interview. The structured portion of the interview is the time to begin building rapport with the interviewee. The structured approach can help establish the relative status of the interview participants and assists in creating a secure feeling for both.

The Semistructured Approach

The semistructured approach begins at about point C of the flowchart. The use of this approach implies your desire to receive information from interviewees in an immediate way—that is, promptly and without rambling. However, it does not imply the use of coercion, abuse, or intimidation. Accusation and confrontation toward interviewees is not appropriate in this mode. With the semistructured approach, try to tune in to what is happening moment by moment. You should be alert for signs that the truth is trying to show itself. Look for patterns signaling deception.

The formulation of questions in the semistructured mode is not materially altered by the interviewee's responses. The questions are partly intended to stimulate the interviewee to exhibit verbal and nonverbal behavior that may be indicative of deception. Follow the "bones" described in Chapter 9 when formulating your questions.

The Nonstructured Approach

At about point F or G of the interview interaction, you may decide to alter your interview strategy and use specific review and persistent encouragement to resolve inconsistencies in the interviewee's story. You will usually reach a strategic deduction while attempting to resolve inconsistencies. The interviewee's hostility or reluctance to provide truthful information might be the basis for a greater intensity of review and encouragement. This turning point requires delicate handling. If you decide prematurely that the interviewee is being deceptive and change your strategy abruptly, you might spark greater reluctance on the part of the interviewee. Between points F and H, after attempting to resolve inconsistencies, you may decide to proclaim clearly your belief in the interviewee's culpability and to begin an interrogation. Proficient interrogators move smoothly and cleverly to help the interrogatee reveal the truth.

PUTTING IT ALL TOGETHER

There is a clear relationship between the levels of intensity, the participant locations, and the three approaches used during the interview process. During the first part of the interview, the investigator simultaneously uses the structured approach and level 1 intensity. As he or she begins to use the semistructured approach, the intensity increases to level 2. Finally, as the investigator attempts to resolve inconsistencies in the interviewee's story, he or she employs the nonstructured approach and intensity levels 3, 4, and 5.

When the participants are in the conversation location, the approach ranges from structured to semistructured. Touching does not occur. The intensity of review and encouragement stays in the general and minimal ranges.

In the moderate location, intensity levels 1, 2, and 3 are used. The distance between the interview participants varies with the intensity of the interaction. When using levels 1 and 2, the investigator maintains a distance of about four feet from the interviewee. With level 3, the distance between participants is about four feet. From points C to G on the polyphasic flowchart (see Figure 9.1), the participants are about four feet apart; from G to J, two to four feet; and from J to K, about two feet. Reassuring touch is not used with levels 1 and 2, but it can be employed with level 3 at a distance of about two feet. In the moderate location, the semistructured and nonstructured approaches are used to formulate questions. Between points F and G, the investigator might announce that there appear to be inconsistencies in the information that the interviewee has provided.

The intimate location is used with intensity level 4. The investigator uses this location to comfort or to confront. *Intimate* implies a closeness between participants that might strengthen rapport and stimulate greater cooperation. Confrontations about inconsistencies take place in this location, as well as the beginnings of interrogation.

REVIEW QUESTIONS

1. What is a key consideration when selecting an interview location?

2. What is personal space, and what might happen if you invade an interviewee's personal space?

3. What is proxemics, and why is it important?

4. What are the three locations, and how are they used in the interview process?

5. Name two uses for the intimate locations.

6. How can you use review and encouragement strategically to uncover the truth?

7. What is the objective of using the various intensity levels of review and encouragement?

8. Is it appropriate to use tactics involving bullying or coercion at the highest intensity level?

9. When should you challenge inconsistencies?

10. What is the goal of the structured approach, and what types of questions are appropriate?

11. When is the semistructured approach used?

12. When does a turning point in strategy occur?

Questions and Questioning

Interviewing is the task of gathering information (Freeman and Weihofen 1972). It is "a process of dyadic communication with a predetermined and serious purpose designed to interchange behavior and involves the asking and answering of questions" (Stewart and Cash 1974, p. 5). Interviewing is best done face to face. There is a complex interaction that takes place during an interview in which there are observations made by both participants as they check and recheck each other's verbal and nonverbal behavior. There is a mutual analysis: the interviewee is scrutinizing the investigator for signs of believability while being observed for patterns of deception. Seasoned interviewers know that luck is merely what is left over after careful planning and preparation. They develop a plan for each interview but remain flexible when applying it. They help interviewees rationalize and save face, thus encouraging their cooperation. To become a proficient interviewer, you will need average intelligence and common sense, a keen power of observation, resourcefulness, persistence, and a tireless capacity for work. Never act in a stern, imperious, or harsh manner. Be guided by your intuition, not guesses or speculations, but be sure your intuition is based on your direct observation and immediate experience.

At a crime scene, locate witnesses and record their identity. Without pressure or suggestion, encourage them to provide a narrative account of their observations. When contacting witnesses later, identify yourself, explain the reason for the contact, and ask the witness to recall everything observed during the period of the crime. The greater the amount of time between the incident and the location of witnesses, the less chance they will be able to report accurately what they observed.

Unobtrusively direct the interview, deciding when to listen, when to talk, what to observe, and so on. In so doing, observe, evaluate, and assess the interviewees, including what they say both verbally and nonverbally, how they say what they say, and what they fail to say. The plausibility of a witness's observation is critical to the overall investigation; therefore, consider the ability of each interviewee to see and hear what was reportedly observed. With overly talkative interviewees who ramble, or with those who tend to wander from the topic, gently and empathically guide them back, redirecting them through leading questions to a discussion of the issue at hand.

Information-gathering interviews need to be based upon fact rather than opinions or feelings. Novice interviewers collect more opinions and feelings than facts (Banaka 1971, p. 100). "Skillful probing differentiates effective [interviewers] from ineffective ones" (Downs et al. 1980, p. 243). Interviewees provide opinions wherever and whenever they can; it is your job to distinguish true factual data from opinionated, emotional comments. Separate observations from interpretations, facts from feelings. If you notice interviewees interpreting facts rather than presenting observed details, avoid being judgmental and pouncing on them. Without pressure or suggestion, encourage them to provide a narrative of their observations regarding the investigative problem. Avoid knowingly bringing into your inquiry any biases or prejudices that might lead to misguided observations and improper evaluation.

QUESTION FORMULATION

Interviewers succeed when they convince their subjects to provide truthful information. It's not a matter of telling, but a matter of selling. Well-crafted questions sell the interviewee on the idea of telling the truth. You need to be a persuader of sorts, using properly phrased questions in a setting and under circumstances that persuade the interviewee to answer honestly. Questions encourage compliance when their design is simple. Make them more specific and complex only after evaluating the interviewee's responses. Aristotle said, "Think as wise men do, but speak as the common people do." Ask questions spontaneously to express ideas in a natural and subconscious manner. Trust yourself to ask properly worded questions while encouraging the subject to cooperate. When appropriate, make your questions specific, definite, and concrete. Vague, general questions permit interviewees to wiggle and squirm away from your desired goal.

Choose your words with care. Words represent partial images, not the total picture. Avoid legal-sounding terms like *homicide, assault,* and *embezzlement.* Misused, they tend to make interviewees unnecessarily defensive. Interviewees welcome the opportunity to respond to questions for which they know the answers, and they feel more free to talk when the topic is familiar. Interview suspects tend to avoid answering questions that make them appear dumb, foolish, or uninformed. When embarrassed or upset over a question, interviewees avoid eye-to-eye contact and may display signs of distress. Some people appear shifty-eyed when they are lying, are planning to lie, or have been asked to reveal private information about themselves.

QUESTION PRESENTATION

A question is a direct or implied request for the interviewee to think about a particular matter. Comments based on assumptions can be regarded as questions if they invite the interviewee to respond. Rather than rely on many questions, allow the interviewee to speak freely. Some interviewees elaborate more readily when asked fewer questions. Once an interviewee decides to talk, you often need only guide the discussion with timely encouragement. Your assumptions, behavior, and method of questioning will, to some extent, determine the interviewee's response and willingness to cooperate. Even your vocabulary could cause embarrassment or fright. Interviewees who lose face because they don't understand your words may become disturbed or insulted, they may feel naked and vulnerable, and they may become judgmental and skeptical (Berne 1974; Harris 1973; *I Understand, You Understand*). Their resentment may cause them to fail to think clearly, to refuse to cooperate, or even to lie. On the other hand, some interviewees will be extremely cooperative in trying to answer all questions even with an interviewer who asks poorly phrased questions based on crude, biased assumptions. By initiating the question-answer pattern, you tell interviewees as plainly as if put into words that you are the authority, the expert, and that only you know what is important and relevant. This may humiliate some interviewees who regard such a pattern as a third-degree tactic. Therefore, phrase your questions carefully, and be sensitive enough to realize when not to ask questions. Noticing the sincerity of your tone of questioning, and how you avoid asking abrasive, leading questions, interviewees will feel less need to be defensive.

Question objectively. Avoid giving the impression that you have taken sides in the investigation. This may be difficult for interviewers who represent certain organizations, such as law enforcement agencies. It is inappropriate for you to register surprise or shock at any statement that an interviewee makes (Woody and Woody 1972, p. 126).

Regard the interview as a conversation, not a cross-examination. "Do not grill the interviewee as a prosecuting attorney might do. Ask questions in a conversational manner, because your purpose is to hold a conversation with someone who has knowledge or has experienced something that you want to know about. Holding a conversation implies a certain amount of give-and-take during the interview. Make sure that you are asking questions and not making statements that do not call for answers" (Downs et al. 1980, p. 286).

Never ask questions in a belligerent, demeaning, or sarcastic manner. Questions that begin "Isn't it true that you . . ." tend to be abrasive and promote defensiveness. Pushing interviewees into a corner where they will have to defend themselves is self-defeating. Do not embarrass interviewees by asking questions that they cannot answer. This will only make them uneasy and will create unnecessary tension. Similarly, asking questions accusingly, suspiciously, or abruptly or asking "trick questions" may arouse fear and defensiveness and will not promote cooperation. All of these tactics are counterproductive.

To emphasize your genuine interest in the details the interviewee has provided and to promote a positive view of your thoroughness, review all details during questioning. This will allow coverage of more specific areas of interest as the need arises. Make it appear that some details are not as clear as they could be, or claim to have missed some meaningful information.

TYPES OF QUESTIONS

Two main types of questions are generally used in interviews: closed questions and open questions. The objective of the inquiry determines the use of closed or open questions. Fewer tactical restrictions apply to using open questions. By tactical restrictions, I mean strategic limitations that might hamper your progress in calling for the truth. Open questions allow for various angles or degrees of considered approach. They can be calculated to emphasize points of the inquiry using various levels of review and encouragement.

Closed Questions

Closed, or closed-ended, questions are specific, offering a limited number of possible responses. Yes or no questions and multiple-choice questions are types of closed questions. Use closed questions at the beginning of an interview to encourage affirmative responses and to put interviewees more at ease.

The yes-no or either-or option of some closed questions limits the scope of responses and options. This can be useful when you want to maintain maximum control over the interview and thereby save some time. They are also handy when dealing with reluctant interviewees who will not give detailed responses. "Insofar as gaining information is concerned, narrow [closed] questions have the advantage of eliciting details." In contrast, "open-ended questions rely almost exclusively on the [interviewee's] unaided ability to recall" (Binder and Price 1977, p. 44). However, the unrestricted use of closed questions will hamper your efforts. "Narrow questions can inhibit the development of rapport. . . . The misuse of narrow questions involves detailed probing before the [interviewee] is ready. People will be willing to provide details, particularly about sensitive subjects, only if they feel comfortable in doing so. Therefore, probing too soon, without first having developed a maximum of rapport, may cause the [interviewee] to feel improperly invaded" (Binder and Price 1977, pp. 44–45).

Open Questions

Open, or open-ended, questions start with *who, where, what, when, how,* or *why.* They cannot be answered yes or no, and they require the suspect to think clearly. Although they create the most distress, they also reveal the greatest amount of information. Open questions help interviews flow. Most open questions ask *what, why,* or *how.*

To learn the cause, reason, or purpose, ask the question *why. Why* questions search out the facts of a situation and probe areas not commonly touched by more complicated questions. There are times, however, when the *why* question creates a threatening situation in which interviewees become defensive. Faced with the question "why," they may feel rejected, misunderstood, or imposed upon. They may withdraw, prevaricate, or hit back with silence that may confuse or frustrate you. Questions beginning with *why* may provoke undue stress because they generate too much challenge. Interviewees generally cannot answer the question "why?" regarding subconscious thinking or behavior. Answering reveals too much of the self, and self-disclosure makes people uncomfortable.

Open questions can help you accomplish several goals:

- Discover the interviewee's priorities, attitudes, needs, values, aims, and aspirations
- Determine the interviewee's frame of reference and viewpoints
- Establish empathic understanding and rapport
- Engage in active listening, stroking, positive regard, and recognition
- Allow and encourage interviewees to express their feelings and reveal facts without feeling threatened
- Promote catharsis, or expression of the interviewee's emotions

Several different types of open questions can be used effectively during an interview. They are discussed below.

Reflective Questions

Reflective questions mirror the subject' comments. They are used to handle objections. You might begin, "Let me see if I've got this straight . . ." or "So, what you're saying is . . ." Once you've responded to the interviewee's concerns, repeat the question that triggered the objection. By removing the obstacle to cooperation, you help the interviewee feel more comfortable responding to your subsequent questions.

Directive Questions

Directive questions are used to direct the interviewee's attention to areas of agreement with the investigator. Interviewees want to know the benefits to themselves of cooperation. A directive question answers this concern: "You do want to get to the bottom of this, don't you?"

Pointed Questions

Pointed, or direct, questions are specific in nature, pointing directly at the goal. They are designed to rouse the interviewee to action. Most of the questions asked in forensic interviews are pointed questions. By asking exactly what is desired, these questions show interviewees that you believe they are ready, willing, and able to respond. This method, which is based on the self-fulfilling prophecy, works most of the time.

Pointed questions might stimulate the physical expression of the interviewee's stress, but they need not be offensive or accusatory. On the contrary, they should be thoughtfully developed and subtly applied to avoid invoking stress and making the subject defensive. You can gently stimulate the interviewee's thinking with pointed, creative questions. For example, if you believe that the interviewee accidentally set a fire, you might ask, "On the day of the fire, how often did you smoke in the storeroom?"

Indirect Questions

Pointed questions are not always appropriate. Indirect questions provoke less stress, less fear, and hence less defensiveness on the part of the interviewee. They help subjects save face and rationalize their behavior by giving them "a universal blessing." For example, you might say, "I've talked to many of the other employees, and they believe that . . . What do you think?" Indirect questions of this nature can help interviewees express their hidden self, their thoughts and feelings, and so on. Indirect questions are often used at the beginning of an interview and as a change of pace during the course of the discussion. They can also be used as diversion questions (see below).

Self-Appraisal Questions

Self-appraisal questions ask the interviewee to evaluate or judge him- or herself. They help the investigator develop a hypothesis about the *who, how,* and *why* of a crime or another incident. Through self-appraisal questions, the interviewer gains a deeper understanding of the interviewee's needs and probes his or her opinion, revealing possible evasiveness and distress. It is almost impossible for a deceptive or evasive interviewee to be consistent in answering self-appraisal questions. To respond deceptively, the interviewee must first think of an answer, decide that the answer would not sound good, and then make up a new story and tell it convincingly.

Diversion Questions

Diversion questions focus on something or someone near and dear to the interviewee. They have two purposes: (1) They lessen tension by distracting the interviewee from a tension-producing issue, and (2) they restore rapport between the subject and the investigator with a direct or indirect compliment. Diversion questions are useful when dealing with highly emotional interviewees. For example, the investigator might say in a matter-of-fact tone, "Now, let's put that aside for a minute. I want to cover another point with you about your view of how the company can improve the security. As I mentioned, part of why I'm interviewing several people is to accomplish two things. First, I would like to get that missing money back and second, I want to prevent this from happening again. Let me ask you, how can such a loss be prevented in the future?" The rambling nature of the question provides time for the interviewee to calm down if the interviewer had pushed some emotional buttons in previous questions.

Leading Questions

Leading questions include some assumption on the part of the investigator. For example, the statement "From what I hear you say, you must have had a rough time in that job last summer" contains an assumption and invites the interviewee to elaborate or explain. Leading questions containing implicit messages can be used to maintain moderate emotional tension in the interview, but they need not be abrasive if thoughtfully constructed. Leading questions can guide the interviewee toward greater cooperation with your investigation. They reflect your assumption that the interviewee can provide useful information. Leading questions can convey the interviewer's acceptance of the individual, thereby enhancing rapport.

Leading questions are usually thought to produce invalid, unreliable answers. This is true when they are carelessly used. Novice investigators sometimes have trouble using leading questions because their tone of voice and related nonverbal signals are not well controlled. Consequently, interviewees may feel condemned when faced with carelessly presented leading questions. Ulterior motives are typically built into leading questions. Use leading questions with the ulterior motive of stimulating conversation and encouraging the interviewee to reveal the truth.

TECHNIQUES FOR EFFECTIVE QUESTIONING

The following guidelines will help you formulate effective interview questions.

- Avoid the third degree.
- Use closed questions when appropriate.
- Use open questions when appropriate.
- Keep your questions simple.
- Avoid ambiguously worded questions.
- Use leading questions properly.
- Ask self-appraisal questions.

- Have the gall to ask tough questions.
- Encourage cooperation.
- Mentally assume an affirmative answer.
- Pursue unanswered questions.
- Identify and challenge deception.
- Handle trial balloons calmly.
- Assume more information is available.

Having the Gall to Ask

Investigators "usually have problems asking tough or embarrassing questions and they may even avoid asking these questions to save themselves from embarrassment. There is no doubt it takes a certain amount of gall to ask someone if he or she stole the money, killed the husband, or got drunk and ran over a neighbor's child" (Downs et al. 1980, p. 288). Conducting an investigative interview requires that you be brave enough to ask questions that would be rude and intrusive in other situations. To justify asking certain questions, participants need to agree that those questions are necessary.

Encouraging Cooperation

Encourage interviewees to provide information even when they have preconceived ideas about their role in the investigation (Kahn and Cannell 1957). If an interviewee has a role in an investigation, it is one of assisting the investigator by providing information that they alone may have. The investigator gleans information picked up by the interviewee who may have seen or heard something of value to the inquiry. By intentionally altering your verbal and nonverbal communication in a positive manner, you stimulate interviewees to respond cooperatively and truthfully (Nirenberg 1963). Encourage them to feel that cooperation enhances their sense of usefulness; in other words, associate cooperation with need fulfillment (Nirenberg 1963). Help the interviewee justify compliance.

When interviewees try to argue that they should not comply, they are indicating that they are at least considering compliance, or they wouldn't argue the point. Even interviewees who show up for a scheduled interview and sit quietly without responding to questions signal that they are considering compliance. Each situation is unique, requiring evaluation (Nirenberg 1963). Assume that reluctant interviewees have some degree of resentment, and ask questions designed to uncover that hidden resentment. An interviewer's concerned attempts to convey compassion to a victim may be enough to encourage someone to share needed information. That someone may be the interviewee's friend or relative who learns of the attempt at compassion.

Refusal tends to be the most resistant response from uncooperative interviewees; most will not resort to violence (Dexter 1970, p. 32). Faced with refusal, display the attitude that the interviewee will decide to cooperate in the future (Wicks and Josephs 1972). When interviewees sense that they can leave if they choose, they often feel trust and faith in you (Bennis et al. 1973, p. 252). Their freedom to leave tends to release any fear that might hinder compliance.

Although most interviewees feel a personal obligation to answer truthfully, that obligation is lessened when the investigator is obviously unskilled in formulating questions. If the interviewee's expectations conflict with the investigator's questioning style, the interviewee may feel frustrated or annoyed. As a consequence, rapport may suffer (Binder and Price 1977, p. 65).

Interviewee reluctance or hostility may indicate avoidance of the topic under investigation, fear of retaliation, or maybe personal involvement in the delinquency. Your task is to guide the subject toward cooperation. Be a successful persuader, convincing interviewees to cooperate with your investigation (Bennis et al. 1973, p. 247). Gain information by strengthening the interviewee's sense of obligation (Bennis et al. 1973, p. 70). If necessary, help the interviewee create a temporary new identity that will allow him or her to move from limited compliance to more complete cooperation.

Such tactics are not negative if your intentions are basically helpful and honorable.

You can encourage cooperation by beginning the interview with simple closed questions that invite a positive response before asking more complex, specific, open questions. By conveying the impression that you need and expect additional facts, you can subtly encourage the interviewee to reveal more information. If you can do so without creating unnecessary tension, imply that you have already obtained considerable information against which you will check the interviewee's responses.

Mentally Assuming an Affirmative Answer

Uncooperative interviewees are willing to terminate an interview as soon as comfortably possible, particularly if they sense that you doubt your own abilities to obtain information. All they need is some encouragement in the form of negatively phrased questions, such as, "You wouldn't happen to know anything about the fire, would you?" Investigators typically shake their head from side to side when asking questions like this.

To avoid receiving negative responses that lead you to a dead end, mentally assume an affirmative answer to a closed question, and ask the next logical question instead. For example, don't ask, "Have you seen or talked with Sam Smith recently?" The interviewee could define *recently* as "within the last several hours" and could answer no, closing off further discussion. Instead, assume that the interviewee *has* seen Smith recently, and ask, "When was the last time you saw or talked with Sam Smith?"

This second question, an open question, cannot be answered yes or no. The interviewee must give a complete response if he or she answers at all. The response you receive will determine the direction of subsequent questions. For example, if the interviewee responds, "I spoke with Sam two days ago," you might ask, "What was Sam wearing when you last saw him? What kind of car was he driving? Who was he hanging around with?" These questions will help you determine Smith's appearance, his means of transportation, and his current associates.

Pursuing Unanswered Questions

There are many reasons why an interviewee might fail to answer a question or might provide an incomplete or nonsensical response. Perhaps the interviewee is preoccupied or distracted and did not hear the question correctly, or perhaps he or she is too overwhelmed by emotion to answer. If your question was poorly worded, the interviewee might not have understood what you were asking. Be patient. Give the interviewee time to think without challenging him or her. Then ask the question again, varying the wording if appropriate. Never ignore an unanswered question and go on to another topic. To go on and leave questions unanswered will only cause you eventual frustration.

Of course, the interviewee might ignore a question because he or she has something to hide. Always maintain a certain amount of unexpressed skepticism. When repeating a question, be alert for possible signals of deception. Be aware of patterns indicating that the truth is emerging. By not answering, an innocent interviewee might hope to avoid discussion of a difficult topic. You can reduce tension by repeating or rewording your question. When the interview touches on sensitive or threatening topics, you may need to restate a question to find a more acceptable form. Some words trigger mental images that may be emotionally painful to the interviewee, causing him or her to block out certain thoughts. Whether you repeat or reword a question depends on the circumstances and how you evaluate your progress in the interview.

There are times when it is useful to ask a mild, modified version of an emotionally loaded question before asking the main question. This warns the interviewee of the emotional question to follow, helping the interviewee prepare for it. At other times, it is necessary to spring emotion-laden questions on the interviewee to reveal any hidden tension.

Never demand an answer to a question. Don't point out that the interviewee failed to answer. Instead, reword your question, and try again. Some interviewees will try to provoke you into challenging them so they will feel justified in storming out of the interview room. Even victims and witnesses of a crime may feel insulted if challenged by a demand to answer a question. By calmly repeating your questions, you signal persistence, patience, and humanity, which strengthen the bonds of interpersonal communication.

Identifying and Challenging Deception

Although we cannot all claim King Solomon's special wisdom, we can at least use our talents as observers to uncover the truth. We can watch for behavioral patterns that indicate possible deception.

A lead-in that introduces a change of topic—for example, "Now I'm going to ask you a few questions about the day the money was missing"—causes some interviewees to nonverbally signal their intent to deceive. They may fidget in their chair, cross their legs or arms, or break eye contact. Any such sign of uneasiness should cause you to question mentally the truthfulness of the answers that follow.

Do not immediately confront or challenge interviewees who display signs of uneasiness prior to or while answering announced questions. To challenge indicates that you have concluded that the topic of the question is bothersome or that the interviewee intends to lie. Instead, ask your question, and note the interviewee's uneasiness for review later. Look for patterns of evasiveness that may indicate deception. When a clear pattern of evasiveness becomes evident, gradually challenge the interviewee. Isolated signs of evasiveness, although important, are not enough to warrant a challenge.

Some degree of unprovoked anxiety may be useful in an interview. Unprovoked anxiety means an uneasiness possibly brought to the interview and not caused by the investigator as some planned effort. That anxiety may be caused by the interviewee's knowledge of someone's personal responsibility. When sensed, that anxiety can be used as the basis of you displaying your humanness and showing you are okay to talk to. You can enhance tension through your use of questions or by commenting about the interviewee's defense mechanisms or sensitivity to certain events. However, insensitive confrontation over conflicting details in the interviewee's story could cause undue tension, evasiveness, and defensiveness, resulting in an unproductive interview.

Handling Trial Balloons

Interviewees sometimes ask "trial balloon" questions. For example, a subject might ask, "Just say I did take the money—what would happen to me?" or "What usually happens to a person who steals merchandise?" These what-if questions may indicate that the interviewee is on the brink of reporting some significant fact.

When the interviewee floats a trial balloon, avoid pouncing on it as an admission of guilt. Instead, calmly respond to the inquiry, and subtly ask questions that encourage the interviewee to tell the truth. What-if questions are used to test the water, so to speak, to see if it is safe. They signal the need for continued patience and persistence; they do not indicate that it is time to charge ahead destructively.

Terminating the Interview

Always assume that more information is forthcoming and that you need only ask appropriate questions and give adequate encouragement. Even when it seems you have reached the termination point—when it seems as though all questions have been asked and answered—continue to assume that the interviewee has more to tell you. You might ask, "What else can you tell me about what happened?" or "What else should I know about this matter?"

At some point, of course, you will need to terminate the interview. You can do this several ways. Even if you have no intention of questioning the subject again, you might announce that a second interview is possible. Or you might make arrangements for a second interview and give yourself time to prepare further. Finally, you might lead into a confrontation by announcing that you believe there are inconsistencies that must be resolved or by specifically accusing the interviewee of the crime. Your next step would be to attempt to gain a confession or an admission of guilt. In most instances, you will probably end the interview and not need to speak with that person again.

REVIEW QUESTIONS

1. What is the objective of interviewing?

2. How can leading questions help you with overly talkative interviewees?

3. How should you respond when the interviewee provides opinions instead of facts?

4. Why shouldn't you ask vague questions?

5. What is a question?

6. Why is it important to ask questions objectively?

7. Is the interview a conversation or a cross-examination? Explain.

8. Give two examples of closed questions.

9. How do most open questions begin?

10. What are two things that open questions can help you do?

11. Name three types of open questions, and give an example of each.

12. How are pointed questions based on the self-fulfilling prophecy?

13. What type of question can help you develop and strengthen rapport?

14. What is one advantage of using leading questions?

15. How do polite social conversations differ from investigative interviews?

16. How does your expectation play a role in gaining truthful information?

17. Why isn't it a good idea to ignore unanswered questions and go on with the interview?

18. How might your questions trigger emotions that block the interviewee's thought process?

19. What is a trial balloon question, and how should you respond to it?

20. Why should you assume that the interviewee has more to tell you even at the end of the interview?

12

Three Case Studies

THE CASE OF THE IMPATIENT GUARDIAN

"You've done some work for us before," the man on the phone said. He identified himself as Investigator Baker, corporation security officer for a large bank. "Could you assist us on a theft case? It involves a loss of $6,000."

"I'd be glad to help," I said. "When do you need me there?"

"Well, tomorrow if you can. We've been working on this for several days and can't figure out what happened to the money."

"Tell me more about the loss."

"He told me that about a week earlier, $6,000 was found to be missing from a shipment of $25,000 between the main bank and a branch office."

"Could the loss be a mistake?" I asked.

"Probably not!"

Investigator Able got on the line and explained that he was a security officer at the bank. He also mentioned that the two men had worked on the theft together for several days before calling me.

The Initial Phase: Precontact

Investigator Able told me that the loss was thought to have taken place in or near the mailroom of the main bank. The money was temporarily stored in a locked drawer before it was taken to be sent via a public courier to a bank branch office. The branch office reported the loss when the shipment of money arrived there and was counted. Inquiries at the branch office and the mailing service convinced investigators Able and Baker that the money must have been stolen from the main office before the shipment was sent. The focus was on seven employees who, because of their knowledge, access, and opportunity, were considered suspects.

After reviewing the case, I identified eight people I wanted to interview. All but one had access to the shipment of money prior to the theft. The other interviewee, Violet, was engaged to marry Sam, another of the bank employees. I did not suspect her in the theft but thought of her as a possible source of useful information. Able and Baker had not interviewed Violet, but they had spoken with each of the others twice.

Based on their interviews with the seven employees, both Able and Baker concluded that most were totally cooperative; Pete and Gary were the exceptions. I had no way to determine how cooperative Violet would be, but I expected that all of the others except Pete and Gary would agree to help with the investigation.

The Initial Phase: Strategic Planning

As an outsider, I often have some advantage over in-house investigators in evaluating the evidence because I'm less affected by emotional power struggles within the organization. In-house investigators, because they are so close to the problem, frequently cannot or do not perceive meaningful details and signals. I suspected that this might be the case in this investigation.

Evaluating Potential Interviewees

Gary and Pete were identified as the prime suspects because of verbal and nonverbal signals noted by the investigators—not so much by what they said, but by how they said it. Investigator Able selected Gary as the probable thief because he was abrupt and overly resistant in answering questions. Investigator Baker, on the other hand, suspected Pete because he saw him as a self-centered wise guy, using a sarcastic manner to deliver pleasant-sounding words. Both were depicted as overly confident and defiant in their actions. These two employees were unshakably convinced that neither they nor anyone they knew had stolen the missing money. One employee seemed to be above suspicion. Investigator Able was convinced that Sam could not have committed the theft. The investigator may have felt that way because he trusted Sam with extra responsibility. As the armed guard, Sam routinely accompanied the bank messenger to deliver shipments of money to be mailed to the branch office.

I evaluated the interviewees, sight unseen, based on information provided by Investigators Able and Baker. By assigning numerical values to particular characteristics, I calculated the chances of gaining truthful testimonial evidence from each interviewee.

Creating an Interview Strategy

Investigators Able and Baker were reluctant to have me interview Violet. They couldn't see the benefit of talking to her. Logically, even though I did not consider Violet a suspect, I knew that because of her relationship with Sam, my interaction with her laid the foundation for my interaction with all other interviewees. But more than that, I used her interview as a symbolic show of my intention to use whatever means necessary to get to the truth of the matter. I wanted to show them, the band of three buddies who trusted each other and would not say anything bad about each other (identified later), that no one was out of bounds with me. I wanted to show everyone the boldness of my pursuit. In addition, I hoped that Violet would be my messenger to the other employees who might ask her about me and the questions I ask.

I didn't completely reveal my thoughts to the investigators because I didn't think they would understand where I was headed. This chess game was difficult enough for me to comprehend, let alone explain it to someone else. In addition, their minds were obviously already made up.

Preparing Psychologically for the Interview

I planned to enter the interviews with an open mind, even though I was told that Pete and Gary were the prime suspects. Determined to put possible misinformation aside, I used positive expectancy in all efforts to gather truthful information.

The Initial Phase: Contact

Introduction and Greeting

Investigator Able accompanied each individual to the interview room but did not enter the room. He knocked, and I opened the door to admit the interviewee. Investigator Able introduced each person to me by their first and last name while using the more formal "Mister" to refer to me. Thus Investigator Able acknowledged a certain status for me that the interviewees tended to maintain throughout the interaction. The formal introduction helped me appear to be more than a mere associate of Investigator Able. It was important for me to be separated from everything that occurred earlier in the investigation.

Seating

Investigator Able made arrangements for me to conduct the interviews in a quiet, comfortable, private room where the interviewees and I would not be disturbed by interruptions or noise. I positioned the chairs in the interview room so that I would face the interviewee and there would be an uncluttered wall behind me. We would be seated about six to eight feet apart at the beginning of the interview. As the interview progressed, I would move my chair to within about four feet of the interviewee, as is typical of most interview situations. The chairs I selected were of similar design and comfort.

Announcing My Objective

Within the first few minutes of each interview, I told each interviewee that the basic objective of the interaction was to find out how the money went missing from the bank and how we might get it back. I did not mention apprehension or prosecution. I mentioned several reasons why, in my experience, people take money. I tried to convey the idea that the person who took the money was probably trying to solve personal financial problems. My experience is that if there is a time to open the door to the truth, it is at this point of discussion, in the first four minutes, when the interviewee is trying to determine whether it is safe to confide in me.

I reviewed the basic facts of the reported loss of $6,000 with each interviewee to ensure each person understood the specific issue under investigation. Interviewees sometimes suspect that an investigation concerns more than the announced issue; they may think the organization is sweeping their house clean, looking for every loss—no matter how small or remote.

Setting the Tone

I consider it vital to set a positive tone within the first four minutes of the interview. My efforts to establish a positive tone in each interview paid off in this case because my image was communicated among interviewees. I have found that if interviewees are treated badly, others learn of it and become reluctant to be interviewed, resentful, or uncooperative.

I saw no justification to treat anyone as though they had stolen the money, even though one or more of them might have been responsible. Certainly, to treat Violet in any way other than as a witness would have been improper.

Using the Structured Approach

During those critical first four minutes of the interaction, after announcing the objective of the interview, I asked the interviewees questions that would be easy for them to answer: spelling of name, date of birth, number of years of employment, current position, education, marital status. These questions gave the interviewees the opportunity to vent some emotional energy and to become more comfortable with the interview. Sometimes I can perceive evasiveness and lack of cooperation in this stage of an investigation. During each interview, I used a couple of dozen hidden persuaders, such as active listening and empathy.

The Primary Phase—Day 1
Violet (10:31 A.M–10:50 A.M.)

Age 24, divorced, employed at the bank for a number of years, good worker. Character good, reputation good, loyalty good, no financial problems known. Girlfriend of Sam. No access to missing money. Her only interview.

After the first four minutes of the interview, I engaged Violet in a conversation designed to determine what, if anything, she knew of the missing money. I asked her whom she thought had stolen the $6,000, and she responded that she didn't know anything about the theft. The bits and pieces of information she had were based on organization gossip. It seems that she didn't learn any details of the theft, not even from her boyfriend, Sam, who was the armed guard who handled the money shipment.

Violet's nonverbal communication indicated that she was cautious in her discussion of what she knew of the bank's loss.

Her actions were stiff and controlled. She seemed to be with-holding information, although she claimed to know few details. She appeared hesitant to answer more than she thought was required, as though she were apprehensive about revealing something.

> **Me:** What's your status with Sam?
> **Violet:** "We're engaged." Without being asked, she offered, "Sam is acting the same as always." Her comment seemed rehearsed.
> **Me:** Do you know of anyone who is having problems and might need money?
> **Violet:** No.

Sherrie (10:59 A.M.–11:36 A.M.)

Age 24, married, employed at the bank for a number of years, good worker. Character good, reputation good, loyalty good, no financial problems known. Had access to missing money; she packed the money shipment of $25,000; did not have keys to drawer in which shipment was stored prior to it being mailed. Cooperative.

As the vault teller who bundled the $25,000, Sherrie affirmed that the shipment was assembled correctly. Beyond what she said, her nonverbal messages indicated that she was thinking clearly, and her movements were smooth flowing as she expressed herself. She recalled details about how the shipment was handled. She told me that Al had probably hand-carried the shipment from the vault to the mailroom, where he locked it in a drawer. She thought Bill could also have been in the area near the money.

It was hard for her to believe that anyone in the bank had stolen the money; she wanted to believe in her coworkers, even though she didn't know them well.

> **Me:** What do you think should happen to the person who stole the money?

Sherrie: I think he should be prosecuted and not just let loose to get away with it. I would like to take a polygraph examination if it would assist in the investigation.

Bill (11:44 A.M.–1:01 P.M.)

Age 24, single, employed at the bank for a number of years, good worker. Character good, reputation good, loyalty good, no financial problems known. Had access to missing money; had keys to storage drawer. Cooperative.

Me: Are you the person who stole the $6,000?
Bill: No.
Me: Do you know who stole the missing money?
Bill: I have no idea who did it. Al hand-carried the money shipment from the vault to the mailroom.

Bill spoke and acted naturally and appeared to be thinking clearly.

Me: Is there anyone you suspect who might have taken that money?
Bill: No one. I can't see how anyone would have had enough time to steal the money; at least a couple of minutes was needed to steal it. There were always two people around that drawer in which the money was locked until being carried to be mailed.
Me: Do you have any suspects?
Bill: None.
Me: Who do you trust? Who, do you think, did *not* steal the money?
Bill: I don't know. I trust no one over another.
Me: Do you think the money was actually stolen, or do you think there's some other reason the money is missing?
Bill: I believe it's stolen based on what I've heard of the details.
Me: What do you think should happen to the person who stole the money?
Bill: I think it should be returned.
Me: Do you think the person who stole the money should go to jail?
Bill: It all depends on the circumstances.

Bill attempted to recall details of what happened on the day of the shipment. He recalled specific times and calculated who probably did what at the time. He declared that he took work breaks with Sam, Gary, and Pete each day. I asked him again about his suspicions.

> **Me:** Do you have any suspects?
> **Bill:** No.
> **Me:** Is there anyone you trust the most?
> **Bill:** No. I don't like what it's doing to us.

Bill was referring to how the theft had broken down the closeness of his coworkers. Bill said he had spoken with a judge recently about polygraph examinations. He asked me several questions before volunteering to take one to assist in the investigation. He wanted to know about the likelihood of erroneous results. He said that he realized that the results might not be admissible in court. Our discussion helped him resolve any doubts he had regarding the polygraph examination.

I conducted the test as a continuation of his interview. In my opinion, based on my evaluation of the results, Bill was apparently truthful when he denied any participation in the theft of the $6,000.

The Primary Phase—Day 2

The day of interviewing ended and the behind-the-scenes chatter began. I had other inquiries to deal with and I could not return for several days. Therefore, the next interviews were conducted two weeks later. The delay did more good than harm, it seemed.

Al (8:29 A.M.–9:05 A.M.)

Older, married, long-time bank employee, trusted. Character good, reputation good, loyalty good, no financial problems known. Had access to money; had keys to storage drawer. Cooperative.

Al had hand-carried the money shipment from the vault to the mailroom and had locked it in the drawer. His workday had ended before the messenger and the guard had taken the money to be shipped.

> **Me:** If you stole the money, it's important to tell me about it. How do you stand on that? Did you steal that $6,000?
> **Al:** Me? No sir! I'm too close to retirement. That's the last thing I would do.
> **Me:** Do you know for sure who did steal that money?
> **Al:** No.
> **Me:** Do you have any suspects even though you don't know for sure who took the money?
> **Al:** The boys here are going to school. No idea. I think it happened at the mailing company or at the branch office. The boys here wouldn't jeopardize their future.
> **Me:** Who do you trust the most of everyone you work with?
> **Al:** Everyone with keys, including some of the boys. I trust Bill the most.

Al voluntarily requested a polygraph examination. He emphasized his contention that the money was probably not stolen at the main bank. He believed that the thief needed a few minutes to open the money shipment bag, steal the money, and replace the seal on the bag. If someone among his fellow employees did steal the money, he said, "that person would have to be a Jekyll-and-Hyde personality."

As he left the interview, Al commented, "I hope it's resolved. I don't take kindly to having everyone around here looking at me as though I did it."

Jan (9:14 A.M.–10:19 A.M.)

Age 20, single, employed at the bank for a couple of years. Character good, reputation good, loyalty good, no financial problems known. Had carried the money shipment with Sam from the organization to the mailing station. Had no access to the money prior to transporting the shipment. Cooperative.

Jan and Sam always transported the money to be shipped. It was Bill or Sam who handed her the money on the day in question. Sam and she "gab" as they transport money. That day they talked mostly about the vacation that Sam and Violet had taken recently; Jan reported that Sam spends most of his time with Violet. Jan voluntarily requested a polygraph examination.

> **Me:** If you are the person who stole the money, it's important to tell me about it and get this thing cleared up.
> **Jan:** No, I did not! No way! Life's too good! I'm happy with my life! I wouldn't want to jeopardize it for anything.
> **Me:** Do you know for sure who did steal the money?
> **Jan:** No, they're all my friends. I've thought of each as a possible but can't think of anyone who would do it. I feel guilty thinking any one of them might. I can't accuse any of them.
> **Me:** Who do you suspect might have stolen the money?
> **Jan:** Pete acts like a seventh grader, but I can't think he stole the money.
> **Me:** Who do you trust the most of your fellow employees?
> **Jan:** Sam and Gary.
> **Me:** What else can you tell me regarding the loss?
> **Jan:** I don't want to think that anyone did it.

After evaluating Jan's polygraph examination, it was my opinion that she was apparently truthful in her denial of participation in the theft.

Sam (10:31 A.M.–11:24 A.M.)

Age 22, single, dating Violet, trusted employee, armed guard with additional duties. Character good, reputation good, loyalty good, no financial problems known. Friend of Gary and Pete; they attended college together, and they socialize outside of work. Had access to the money. Cooperative.

In Sam's interview, as in the others, I used a combined approach involving structured and semistructured questions. My intention was to prompt the interviewee to exhibit verbal and nonverbal signals regarding his truthfulness. I've given the most complete account of Sam's interview to illustrate my style and some important details of the procedure I used.

In addition to the semistructured questions asked of everyone else, I asked Sam what his major studies were at college. He told me he had studied engineering and accounting.

> **Me:** What type of work do you do at the bank?
> **Sam:** I work with inventory and car maintenance, odd jobs, and I'm the armed guard accompanying money shipments.
> **Me:** It's important to get this matter cleared up, Sam. I'm asking everyone the same things, and I'd like you to work with me to resolve this issue of the missing $6,000. If you're the person who took the $6,000, it's important to get it straightened out and clear things up. How do you stand on this loss, Sam? Did you steal that $6,000?
> **Sam** (shaking his head): No.

I did not ask this question in an accusatory way, but in an open, neutral way without assuming that Sam was the thief. My delivery of the question was intended to draw out any uneasiness and to reveal evasiveness. Nonverbal signals take place in about a hundredth of a second. I have to give the interviewee my undivided attention to sense such signals, and I must do so without being obvious about it.

> **Me:** Do you know for sure who did take that money?
> **Sam:** No idea.
> **Me:** Do you have any suspicions of who might have taken that money even though you don't know who did it for sure? I'm not asking you to point fingers or anything like that. I'm wondering if anyone has done anything or said anything that causes you to think they might have taken the money.
> **Sam:** No. No one I associate with did it.

When I asked Sam if he knew that the polygraph examination was being made available to everyone in this investigation, he responded that he thought the accuracy of polygraph results was questionable, and he quickly asked me why his girlfriend had been called in for questioning. This snap question seemed like a counterblow from a defensive stance. He presented the question to show that he was protective of Violet, but his behavior indicated that he was trying to avoid the topic of the polygraph examination. I didn't want to give him a reason to walk out of the interview, so I told him that because Violet knew everyone involved in the investigation, it seemed appropriate to ask her if she noticed anything that might be useful to the inquiry. In line with the preceding interaction, I repeated the "Suspicion" question.

> **Me:** Sam, do you have anyone you suspect as a possibility?
> **Sam:** No one I associate with could have done it!

With this diversion question, the potential heat of Sam's protectiveness regarding Violet (in reality, probably a self-protection effort) disappeared so that it would not interfere with my progress.

> **Me:** Who do you trust that you think would not have taken that money?
> **Sam:** There's only one single person, and that's Al, who runs the mailroom in the mornings.
> **Me:** What kind of person do you think did this thing?
> **Sam:** I don't know. It's hard to say. It all depends.
> **Me:** On what?
> **Sam:** I don't know! That's a hard question, hard to make a judgment. I've never known anyone to take anything.
> **Me:** What do you think should happen to the person who actually did steal that $6,000?
> **Sam:** I suppose whatever the law says should be carried out.
> **Me:** How about jail?
> **Sam:** I would imagine if that's what it involves.
> **Me:** Why do you think someone would steal that money?
> **Sam:** For the same reasons as you said—to solve problems with finances and things like that.

Me: Is there any reason for anyone to say they think you took the money? Anything you may have said or done that could have mislead anyone to think you're the one who got that money?

Sam: I didn't take it, and I'm acting the same. They shouldn't say that.

I thought to myself, *That's interesting. Violet said something similar.*

Me: Is there any reason for your fingerprints to be on the shipment that was short the $6,000?

Sam (quickly and defensively): I carry money around the bank every day all around. Heaps of it, both loose and bundled.

Me: Any reason for your fingerprints to be on the paper straps which were around the money from which the $6,000 was taken?

Sam: No.

Me: Do you mind if the investigation extends beyond the organization and into your financial affairs?

Sam: No problem. Tell me more about the polygraph examination.

Sam's response seemed to be a way for him to stop the discussion of his finances. Was this a defensive move, perhaps?

As I was explaining about the function of the polygraph, Sam interrupted me.

Sam (challengingly): What if I don't take it?

Me: Well, you can answer that for yourself. There will be assumptions, certainly. If everybody takes the polygraph examination except one, then the person who doesn't may seem a likely suspect. If you took the money, the examination will show that.

Sam (with a chip on his shoulder): If I don't take it, then you're saying I took the money?

Me: Not at all. You decide. It's available to everyone. Take it or not, it's your choice, you decide! I'm just making it available to everyone to help clear up this matter.

Sam: I don't want to take it then!

Me: Okay. . . . I think we've covered everything for now. I may want to talk with you again.

Sam (as he was leaving the interview room): I'm sorry about not taking that polygraph examination, but I'm not comfortable about it.

Me: That's no problem. Think over what we've talked about, and if you want to take the examination or if you have anything else to talk about, mention it to Investigator Able later. Have a good day, and thanks for your cooperation.

Sam had chewed gum throughout the interview, and his answers were guarded. He appeared pale, and his young healthy body seemed to drag as he left the interview room.

At this point, it was my opinion that Sam was involved in the theft, but to reveal my opinion to Sam then would have been premature and self-defeating. I also thought it necessary to withhold my opinion from Investigators Able and Baker until I had completed all of the interviews that day. I couldn't be sure how many employees were involved in the theft, and I didn't want the investigators to accuse anyone prematurely. They probably wouldn't do such a thing, but I wanted to be sure. Sometimes even a look will give the investigator away.

Gary (12:27 P.M.–1:19 P.M.)

Age 22, single, bank handyman. Good character, good reputation, good loyalty, no financial problems known. Friend of Pete and Sam. Had access to money. Had been reluctant to cooperate earlier in the investigation; seemed convinced that the loss was a mistake, not theft. Indignant.

After I explained the objective of the investigation and asked the background questions, I began using the semistructured approach.

Me: Have you ever been arrested?
Gary: No.
Me: Do you have any friends who have ever been arrested?
Gary (looking away): Not that I can think of. . . . My sister-in-law's brother was in trouble.

I reviewed the generally known facts of the reported theft, then continued with my questions.

> **Me:** I'm asking everyone the same things in an effort to determine what happened to the missing money. If you're the person who caused that $6,000 loss, it's important to tell me about that and to get this thing cleared up. How do you stand on this, Gary? Are you the person who stole that money?
>
> **Gary:** No. (Adding quickly) I learned of the loss the week after it happened. Bill asked me if I knew about the missing money. That was the first I learned of it.
>
> **Me:** Well, then, do you know for sure who did steal that money?
>
> **Gary** (shaking his head): No, I don't.
>
> **Me:** Knowing for sure who did it is one thing, but having suspicions is something else. Who do you suspect did this thing even though you don't know for sure? Is there anyone who, because of what they did or said, causes you to be somewhat uneasy and maybe think they could be involved? Keep in mind that I'm not asking you to point fingers or anything because that wouldn't be fair.
>
> **Gary:** They're all my friends being questioned, and I can't suspect them.
>
> **Me:** Of all the people who had access to the missing money, who do you think could not have stolen that money?
>
> **Gary:** Bill, Al, Sam, and Pete. I trust them a lot; we do things together outside the bank.
>
> **Me:** Do you think the money was actually stolen, or do you think there's some other explanation for the loss?
>
> **Gary:** I don't know. At first, I thought it was bookkeeping error, but now it looks like theft.
>
> **Me:** When it's determined who actually did take that $6,000, what do you think should happen to that person?
>
> **Gary:** I don't know, reprimanded and terminated, maybe court. But court would mean bad press for the bank.
>
> **Me:** How about jail for that person?
>
> **Gary** (smoothly and without hesitation): I should think so!
>
> **Me:** Polygraph examinations are available to those who decide to volunteer for them. Examinations are considered to be a valuable aid to investigations.
>
> **Gary:** No, thank you. I've been an honest, hardworking employee, and you should take my word for it that I didn't steal that money.

I didn't take it! I have a background in electronics, and I don't think polygraphs work.

Me: Well then, is there any reason for anyone to say that you took the money? Anything that you did or said that could have misled anyone to think you could be involved in any way in the theft?

Gary: No, I don't think so. I didn't take it.

Me: What kind of person do you think did steal that money?

Gary: Investigator Baker said it could be an honest, upstanding person. Someone who is angry with the organization.

Me: What would cause someone to take that money?

Gary: I don't know.

Me: Is there any reason for your fingerprints to be on the money straps found in the money shipment bag when it was opened at the branch?

Gary (emphatically): Oh, no!

Me: Can you think of anyone who could have been involved in the theft?

Gary: I can't imagine who it is or that it even happened here.

As Gary left the interview room, he was smug. He seemed to be trying to give the impression that he and his associates did not steal the missing money. As he was about to leave, he told me that he always wanted to become a PI (private investigator). He wanted to know if the job is glamorous and if I liked doing it. I commented briefly that there's some satisfaction in assisting in situations where help is needed and where a matter can be cleared up. I viewed the exchange as Gary's way to stroke me emotionally, to help soothe the open wounds caused by his determined reluctance to comply totally.

As Gary was leaving, I asked him to consider what we had discussed, and I told him that if he thought of anything else, to let Investigator Able or me know. I thanked Gary for his cooperation as he left, even though he had been belligerent and arrogant throughout the interview.

Pete (2:13 P.M.–3:24 P.M.)

Age 22, single, bank handyman. Good character, good reputation, good loyalty, no financial problems known. Friend of Gary and Sam. Had access to the money. Had been reluctant to cooperate earlier in the investigation; seemed convinced the loss was a mistake, not theft. Has an influential relative in the community and used his relative's status as his own.

After I established the objective of the interview and asked the structured questions, Pete said, "This interview is a learning experience for me." He smirked as he spoke, and his posture was challenging. He added sarcastically, "Gee, I've never talked to an FBI agent before." His manner conveyed a subtle put-down. He knew that I wasn't with the FBI at the time of the interview. It seemed his way to sarcastically poke at me and try to put me in my place.

As a prelude to the first semistructured question, I briefly reviewed the case. I told Pete that someone had probably used keys to enter the locked drawer to get at the money shipment in the mailroom. As I was speaking, Pete took out his keys, dangled them in two fingers for about ten seconds to be sure I saw them, and then dropped them on the table dramatically. I didn't comment on the keys but continued with my comments:

Me: Now, if you're the one who stole that $6,000, it's important to tell me about it and get this thing cleared up. How do you stand on that? Are you the one who stole that money?
Pete (shaking his head): No.

Pete squirmed in his chair as I made notes and nothing was said. He looked at the polygraph instrument on the table next to him.

Me: Do you know for sure who actually did steal that money?
Pete: I have no idea.
Me: Even though you don't know for sure who did take that money, do you have anyone in mind who you think may have taken the money because of what they did or said?
Pete (crisply and impatiently): There's really nothing I have on that; I really don't think anyone from the bank took it, to tell you the truth.

Me: Well, then, who do you trust the most? Who do you think was not involved in that theft?
Pete: Gary, Bill, Sam, and Al.

I asked Pete about a pair of pliers that we thought might have been used to reseal the money shipment bag after the $6,000 was removed and before it was mailed to the branch office. Pete knew of the pliers, but he denied having used them at any time. He commented, "It's a far shoot to think that the pliers and where they were found have any meaning." Another put-down, I thought. He seemed to be evaluating my questions and giving them a negative assessment.

Me: Is there any reason for your fingerprints to be on any of the paper found in the pouch when it was opened at the branch office?
Pete: No!
Me: It seems the person who took the money may have done so by getting into the drawer in the mailroom that held the money shipment. Do you have a key to fit that drawer?
Pete (removing keys from a clip on his belt): Here, I have a key that fits all the drawers in that area.
Me: Is there any reason anyone might say they saw you taking something out of the mailroom into the baling room on the day of the loss? [The baling room may have been where the money shipment was opened and resealed with a fresh seal.]
Pete: No.
Me: Now that we've talked about this and some of the important things involved, I'm still interested in who you think might have done this thing. Pete, do you have any thought as to who might have taken that money?
Pete: No, no question marks. Gary, Bill, Sam, or I did not take that money; we have all had lots of opportunity, but didn't.
Me: Let's assume that the person who actually did steal the money was caught and there was no doubt who did it. If that person were here standing before you, what would you say to him or her?
Pete (quickly and smoothly): It's not right! Pay it back!
Me: Do you think that person should go to jail?
Pete: Yes, whatever the law says.
Me: Even if it's Sam, Gary, Bill, or Al?
Pete (firmly): Prosecute!

Me: Isn't that kind of harsh?

Pete: Yes, but they know better.

Me: I'm making the polygraph examination available to everyone in this case. I'm not soliciting or requiring anyone to take the testing, but I am making it available to everyone who wants to volunteer for it. Have you ever taken a polygraph examination before?

Pete: No. I think nervousness may affect the test. No thank you.

Me: What kind of person do you think did steal that money?

Pete: Someone who needs money.

I terminated the interview, and as Pete left the interview room, I commented, "It would be helpful to resolve this matter regarding you, Sam, and Gary. Why not meet with those guys to talk over what happened in your interviews. I'd like you to think about the polygraph." "Yeah! Sure! You bet!" he said, but his tone implied, *Don't hold your breath, fella.*

The Terminal Phase

At the end of the second day of interviews, a police officer asked Gary, Sam, and Pete for their full cooperation, and they consented. I wasn't sure whether I would be involved in the inquiry any longer, until I learned from Investigator Able that he had contacted the three men to verify that they were going to cooperate. They would, they said.

At the end of the second day, I told Investigators Able and Baker that I thought Sam had probably stolen the $6,000. I gave my opinion knowing that there was no guarantee that Gary, Pete, and Sam would agree to undergo polygraph examinations. At that time, the end of the second day, I really didn't know if I would be asked to return to continue the inquiry. My ego dictated that I at least announce to Investigators Able and Baker that I thought Sam stole the money. They both were reluctant to hear my view since they had committed themselves to the opinion that Sam could not be the culpable. They did not argue or refute my view and I left that day convinced that Sam was the thief. The next day Investigator Able called to ask me to continue the inquiry.

The Follow-Up Phase

During his interview two days earlier, Al had volunteered to undergo a polygraph examination. During the test on the morning of the third day, I asked if he was the person who had stolen the $6,000. He said, "No." He added that he had hand-carried the money shipments for mailing for many years.

"Do you know who actually stole the $6,000?" I asked.

"No, sir!" He added that he thought the theft took place at the mailing company or at the branch office that received the shipment.

After evaluating his polygraph examination, it was my opinion that Al was apparently truthful when he denied participating in the theft of the missing $6,000.

Later that afternoon, I conducted polygraph examinations of Pete and Gary. In my opinion as the polygraphist, both men were apparently truthful when they proclaimed they did not steal the $6,000.

Next, I turned my attention to Sam, who had also volunteered to undergo a polygraph examination. My evaluation of the results suggested to me that Sam's denial of involvement in the theft was apparently not truthful.

I explained the results of the examination to Sam, and he made a verbal confession of stealing the $6,000. Sam and I created the following written statement based on his verbal confession. He then read, said he understood, and signed a handwritten statement in which he declared that he had some of the stolen money hidden in his car.

> **Dear Mr. Able:** About 3:15–3:20 on [date], I removed the [branch name] mail pouch from the mailroom to the baling room. I was there for five minutes with the pouch, and I removed the seal. I removed three packs of $20 bills, amounting to $6,000 total. I stole that money to cover personal debts that accumulated for me. I spent about $2,000, and I have about $4,000 in my car at this time which I will return to you immediately. I got the seal I used to reseal the pouch from

purchasing. The pliers I used were in purchasing. I took them to the baling room with me to reseal the pouch after I stole the $6,000.

I am sorry for stealing the $6,000 from the [branch name] pouch, and I want to repay the money I spent. Please understand that I'm sorry and that I will never do anything like this again. Please know that I am under financial pressure and that is why I stole that money from [bank name].

Mr. Yeschke has treated me fairly today. No one has promised me anything or threatened me in any way to make this statement.

The above is the truth.

I called in Investigator Able to witness Sam's signature, and a tacit admission was obtained using the following procedure:

- The accusation must be made in the presence of the defendant.
- The defendant must have understood that he was being accused of complicity in a crime.
- The statement must be such as would naturally provoke a denial from one similarly situated.
- The circumstances must have been such as to afford the accused an opportunity to act and speak freely.
- The person accused must have remained silent or made an evasive or equivocal reply short of a total denial.
- The language of the accusation must be shown in its entirety and in the words used by the accuser.
- If the accused makes a denial in toto, neither the accusation nor the denial is admissible.
- After obtaining a verbal or written admission or confession, ask the subject to sit for a minute while you get your supervisor to come in to verify that you have covered everything properly. Or, you might say you are going to bring a secretary in so that he or she understands what your report will contain.

- Before bringing the third person into the room, instruct the third person to just stand or sit quietly in the room with you and the subject while you do all the talking.
- Upon entering the room, situate the third person so that you can read to him or her. Introduce the third person to the subject.
- Talk to the third person directly while the subject looks on. Clearly stare to the third person that you and (name of subject) put the statement together. Say, "I'm going to read this to you so that you understand what we put together." Then, just before reading the statement, turn toward the subject to state, "If I say anything that is not accurate and correct, please let me know." Then, say something like: "We discussed each part of the statement as we put it together. I read each part of it to (name of subject) as we put it together. Now (name of subject), as I read this, be sure it is clear; if there is anything that we need to change, add or correct, let me know."
- Read the statement to the third party. Tell the third person something like: "I read this to (name of subject) and then I gave it to him to read. He appeared to read it. I asked him if it was clear for him. He said, 'Yes!' I asked him if we should add anything. He said, 'No!' I asked him to write 'The above is true' at the bottom of the page and I asked him to put his name at the bottom, which he did. I asked him if it was true and correct and he said, 'Yes.'"
- To the subject say, "Now (name of subject), is there anything you would like to add to this (motioning to the statement)? Any correction we need to make on it? Anything we should add to it at this time?"
- To the third person say, "He wrote the above is true and he put his name here (showing on the statement where the subject signed and wrote the above is true). I signed here as a witness and put the date and time here (pointing to the statement appropriately as the subject watches)."

Generally, as I read the statement to the third person, the interrogatee is quiet without objecting. His agreement with my comments is implicit in his quietness. He implies his acceptance of my comments regarding his statement by saying nothing. He does not object or refute my narrative. Because he does not express or declare objection to my comments, he is giving unspoken approval to my comment. His tacit acknowledgment that what I said is correct and true is reflected by so doing.

Quietly, I suggested to Investigator Able that we should locate and confiscate the gun that had been issued to Sam for his duties as bank guard. That done, Sam led Investigator Able and me to his new sports car, which was parked across the street from the bank. Sam removed a paper bag containing $3,580 in $20 bills—all that was left of the bank's missing $6,000.

After reviewing my observations, evaluations, and assessments of the eight interviewees, it was my opinion that Sam had acted alone in the theft of the $6,000. I also believed that the other interviewees had no specific knowledge of the theft. Because of loyal friendship and pride, Pete and Gary had unintentionally created a "smoke screen" behind which Sam had hidden. I learned later that Pete and Gary were so convinced that Sam did not steal the money that the three had intentionally banded together to oppose anyone in authority who would even imply that any of them might have stolen the money.

If interviewees intentionally try to anger or placate the investigator, they are probably being defensive, but if they anger the interviewer merely because of their spontaneous behavior, then they are working from a position of confidence and arrogance, showing their hostility to authority and their dislike of their situation. In the case of Pete and Gary, their behavior aggravated the bank investigators and drew their attention to them as the most likely suspects. Their arrogant defiance was consistent and not phony.

REVIEW QUESTIONS

1. How did human needs interfere in this inquiry?

2. How were the in-house investigators misled by the behavior of two of the suspects?

3. Were Pete and Gary trying to protect Sam?

4. What verbal and nonverbal clues led the investigator to the solution?

THE CASE OF THE FALSE ALLEGATION

Background

The following case involves the interrogation of a thirteen-year-old girl, Kathy, who had alleged that her natural father, Michael, had sexually molested her. She later recanted her story. The authorities thought she was lying when she backed away from her allegation. Maintaining her dislike for Michael and seeing that the authorities were convinced of her original allegation, she claimed once again that he had molested her—an allegation that he denied. By the time I became involved in the case, the authorities were frustrated and confused by Kathy's conflicting stories, but they were still obligated to pursue the truth.

Kathy agreed to undergo a detection-of-deception examination. During the preliminary interview, she still asserted that Michael had molested her. However, the polygraph examination indicated that she was apparently lying when she claimed to have had sexual intercourse with her father.

The Gentle Interrogation

Without telling Kathy that it was apparent to me that she had been lying, I tried to ease gently into a confrontation. I could have merely reported my opinion, but I wanted a confession from her. She was capable of making up stories, and I didn't want her to make up anything about how I had treated her. I didn't announce my knowledge of her deception until we had spoken for some time and had developed a rapport. Determining her veracity was only part of my mission. My main objective was to have her own up to the truth and stick with it. Her voluntary and believable confession was needed to stop the prosecution of her father.

> **Me:** Your evaluation is that he was treating you like a three-year-old?
> **Kathy:** Uh-huh.
> **Me:** And he didn't give you much human warmth, then? Is that right?
> **Kathy:** Yeah, he was always looking down at everything and me!
> **Me:** Treated you different than the other kids?
> **Kathy:** Yeah, well, in a way! Me and my brother that died. He treated us the same way. He treated my other brother, the one that would have been his nephew, anyway, really special. Uh-huh.
> **Me:** Really special! Oh, he did?
> **Kathy:** Uh-huh!
> **Me:** You could feel that?
> **Kathy:** Uh-huh!
> **Me:** Yeah, okay. Kathy, we were talking before about the area of sexual contact. You mentioned to me before about seeing in the newspaper how a father had his kids taken away from him.
> **Kathy:** Oh, yeah. Something like that.
> **Me:** Something like that.
> **Kathy:** Yeah, something like that. Yeah.
> **Me:** About when was that? Was that this year?
> **Kathy:** Yeah! I think so, anyway. It was awhile ago!
> **Me:** Okay, but that gave you the idea to give that phony story about the sex thing, is that right?
> **Kathy:** Yeah.
> **Me:** So, let me continue with how he treated you. You said he treated you like dirt. All he wanted was to have you clean his house and get his beer, and so forth?
> **Kathy:** Uh-huh.
> **Me:** Any love, any affection, any warmth, any real true feelings at all?
> **Kathy:** No! He often said . . . he would give me a hug and said he loved me, but it came off with no feeling! It was really cold, and you could tell he didn't mean it.

Me: Well . . .

Kathy: He only did that when my ma was around!

Me: So, just to show her, to put on an act or something?

Kathy: Yeah.

Me: Okay. So, let me ask you, do you really think that he loves you?

Kathy: No!

Me: You're convinced of that?

Kathy: Yes!

Me: Okay! Would you have given this false story about him if you thought he loved you?

Kathy: I might have! With all the stuff he's done and everything, but I don't know!

Me: Let's cover a couple of things he's done. All right? All the things he's done . . . some things are hard to put into words, but let's cover what you know about what he's done, all right? Particularly to your ma! You said to me earlier that you don't think that he does have any fondness or feelings for her, then?

Kathy: Nah.

Me: You don't think he loves her?

Kathy: Nah, not really! It's the way he acts towards her. She really likes him a lot—loves him I guess you could say.

Me: Uh-huh.

Kathy: I think she's kind of blind to the way he treats her!

Me: Uh-huh.

Kathy: He treats her like garbage, too! I mean he comes home with the same routine: "Hi, I'm home. Get me a beer." Then he goes and sits down! Then, you know, he gives my mom a kiss, but you can tell he doesn't mean it cause he's looking away, and he doesn't even look at her.

Me: Okay. How has he hurt her?

Kathy: Just by acting this way to her. They get into physical fights a lot, too! I've had to break them up out of a couple!

Me: Is that right? Hit each other, do they?

Kathy: He hits her mostly! He's tried to kill her before!

Me: Oh, he has?

Kathy: He's gotten on top of her and tried to strangle her, and I've had to pull him off her, you know, and that hurts her a lot!

Me: You feel bad about that?

Kathy: Yeah! She's tried to kill herself! Once! She was planning on it, anyway!

Me: Uh-huh.

Kathy: During one of these fights, she said, he was thinking of walking out, he said. She said, if you're leaving, there's no sense in my living, then. She ran into the kitchen to get a knife to kill herself with. I stopped her from that, too. He would never have stopped her.

Me: Uh-huh.

Kathy: He was just watching her. He didn't care!

Me: Uh-huh. So, he doesn't really care too much about her?

Kathy: No!

Me: Yeah, and how does all this make you feel now?

Kathy: Like he doesn't really love her at all, you know. If she's going to kill herself, if he's not going to live with her any more. And he doesn't even care. He just stands there and watches her. He doesn't even try to stop her.

Me: So, that causes you to feel, then, that he doesn't care about her, and she might hurt herself because she really likes him.

Kathy (tearfully): Yeah!

Me: Is that right?

Kathy: Yeah! Uh-huh.

Me: Can you sense that she might hurt herself?

Kathy: Yeah! I mean, she probably would if, you know, if he's not going to stop her, and like when they're fighting, he's not going to stop her, so I have to stop her. She's not going to automatically quit.

Me: You feel a responsibility?

Kathy: Yeah!

Me: To help her?

Kathy: Yeah!

Me: And so, by giving this phony story you were trying to help her?

Kathy: Yeah, I guess so, to get him out of her life! So she wouldn't hurt herself, I guess.

Me: Okay. And that's why you were giving that story about sexual intercourse and so forth?

Kathy: Yeah!

Me: Okay, okay! Well, it's different, you know, when you look at it that way. It's different than being nasty. I mean, you're not trying to be nasty. You're trying to be helpful! I mean, you're doing something in love for your mom? You follow what I'm trying . . . ?

Kathy: Yeah, I guess so!

Me: Is that correct now?

Kathy: Yeah!

Me: Are you a nasty person?

Kathy: No!

Me: Okay. So, whatever you did, then, on this phony story about sex with Michael, whatever you did there was an act of love for your mom?

Kathy: Yeah.

Me: Is that fair to say?

Kathy: Yeah.

Me: Okay, okay now. I guess what we need to talk about, too, is whether you're sorry for going through the story, the phony story, or are you not. You don't have to be one way or the other. I just want to check with you, all right? How do you feel now? You know you didn't pass your polygraph examination.

Kathy: Yeah, I know that!

Me: All right! And how old are you now?

Kathy: Thirteen.

Me: Thirteen now. Okay. Let me get back to the question. How do you feel now about making that decision to give the phony story? How do you feel about that now? I mean, we found out about that, you and I.

Kathy: Yeah!

Me: You and I talked about that.

Kathy: In some ways, I'm sorry; in some ways, I'm not! I'm sorry that it's gone this far, and all these people are working so hard to get it into court, and it's not even true.

Me: Uh-huh.

Kathy: You know, and then the way I'm not sorry is that all the crap he's pulled, I mean he deserved it!

Me: Okay, okay. I'm not looking for you to be one way or the other! All right!

Kathy: Uh-huh.

Me: As I've said before, it's not up to me to decide. I'm not to judge anything. I just want to work with you. All right? I'm just looking for you to tell me how you feel. So, I hear you say that he's pulled a lot of crap, and he deserves all the hassle you've given him?

Kathy: Yeah. He's given us twice as much as I've given him in the past couple of months.

Me: Okay, all right. So, tell me more about how you feel now, now that you are getting the story out. You're telling the straight scoop, right?

Kathy: Yeah!

Me: What else do you feel?

Kathy: Well, I'm upset with myself for going this far, really! In a way!

Me: Are you?

Kathy: Yeah! Going this far with it to take a polygraph test and then flunking it!

Me: You know you flunked it, right?

Kathy: Oh, yeah!

Me: Yeah, okay, there's no doubt about it, right?

Kathy: Yeah.

Me: Now, during the test, just let me ask you, I could see you weren't giving me your full cooperation. You were trying some funny stuff in there with me. How were you thinking? How were you functioning in there? You were trying some things? And what were you thinking about during the testing?

Kathy: Trying to be as calm as I possibly could.

Me: Uh-huh.

Kathy: Act normal.

Me: Okay, you were doing some things in there to try and throw me a curve. I could see that, and I know that. And I'm not asking you if you were or not, because I can see that. But I'm just asking, what were you thinking when you were doing this? I'm not going to hold it against you, that's no problem! You were trying to protect yourself, I know that. What were you thinking when you were doing that?

Kathy: Just to pass it, you know!

Me: Just to pass it?

Kathy: Yeah, to throw the machine off.

Me: To throw it off a little bit? Yeah!

Kathy: Yeah!

Me: What were you doing? What were you doing to throw it off?

Kathy: Really, just act the same throughout to cover it up real quick, you know!

Me: Uh-huh. Well, what did you do physically?

Kathy: Physically?

Me: Yeah! Muscles or breathing or whatever? You know?

Kathy: I can't even remember if I did anything.

Me: It looks like you did something on your breathing; you were changing your breathing! What were you doing there?

Kathy: I was trying to catch my breath. I was having a little hard time breathing.

Me: Oh, yeah?

Kathy: Yeah!

Me: How else did you feel on the testing?

Kathy: Just, you know, tell a lie, and make it look like the truth!

Me: So, you were trying to make it show it to look like the truth? What were you trying to do to make it look like the truth?

Kathy: Just act real calm and cool!

Me: I want to be sure I have this recording as part of the report. So what I'm saying is, I'm looking to have you explain your feelings, your thoughts. That's what we're talking about, about Michael— Michael and the things you felt in your relationship over the past thirteen years. You already mentioned a certain amount of hassle, anger that you had. What else would you be angry about with him? What else made you angry with him?

Kathy: Mom!

Me: Just about your mom, and so forth?

Kathy: Yeah!

Me: Because she went to get a knife one time, and he tried to choke her another time. He doesn't seem very thoughtful. He doesn't seem like he loves her?

Kathy: Uh-huh. If she was having a nervous breakdown, he wouldn't care. He'd just grab a beer or something, you know?

Me: Okay, he just doesn't care; you said he just doesn't care?

Kathy: Uh-huh. His main idea of punishment for kids, too, is that if they do something accidentally—and if you break something and stuff—it is to hit them and ground them for about a month.

Me: Is that right?

Kathy: Yeah! He says that if they ever smart off to you, just give them a big whack, and then they won't talk about it for a week.

Me: Uh-huh.

Kathy: That's his idea of punishment.

Me: Uh-huh.

Kathy: My mom is not like that, though!

Me: No! But so he has done that sort of thing to you?

Kathy: Uh-huh.

Me: Has he grounded you a lot?

Kathy: Yeah!

Me: How did you feel about that?

Kathy: Well, there's nothing I could do about it! I mean, if I was grounded, if I went against it, I'd just get it worse the next time.

Me: Okay. Let me ask you now, Kathy, as far as you're concerned, do you think he deserved all this treatment by police and authorities and so forth? Do you think he deserved this now? I mean, did he have it coming to him?

Kathy: Most of it, I mean. In my book, he had it coming to him anyway.

Me: Okay. Anything else that should be coming to him? Well, what do you think should happen to him? Now?

Kathy: I don't know. I don't know much about the law or nothing, but I wish my mom would wise up to the ways he treats her.

Me: Uh-huh.

Kathy: You know, but I wised up about it a long time ago.

Me: Yeah! How old were you when you first realized what he was doing?

Kathy: I was about ten or so!

Me: About ten or so?

Kathy: Uh-huh.

Me: What happened there that kind of turned you on to the kind of guy he is?

Kathy: I just started paying more attention to him, how he was acting around my ma, and how he was acting around me.

Me: Uh-huh.

Kathy: And how many fights they got into.

Me: Yeah!

Kathy: Stuff like that.

Me: Yeah, okay!

Kathy: How many times he kicked my dog, and everything else.

Me: Oh, you have a dog he kicked?

Kathy: Yeah, if my dog won't come as soon as he says so. My dog's kind of hard of hearing and old. My dad will kick him.

Me: Ah.

Kathy: He'll say, "You dumb dog," and he'll give him a big kick. My dog is pretty old as it is!

Me: I see! So he really doesn't have any feeling for the dog, either.

Kathy: Not that I can see!

Me: Is there anything good about Michael that you can comment on, anything good about him?

Kathy: Sometimes when he decides to be nice, he can be pretty easy to get along with.

Me: I see.

Kathy: But that isn't that often that he is really that easy to get along with.

Me: What makes you the most angry?

Kathy: What makes me the angriest?

Me: About him, yeah!

Kathy: Everything, really!

Me: Everything he does, huh?

Kathy: Yeah, I mean, his actions, how he treats people in general!

Me: Okay, so he's not a nice guy, then.

Kathy: No.

Me: You first got your idea about the phony story about having sex with Michael . . . this was about when? You said it was about this year?

Kathy: Yeah!

Me: Uh-huh.

Kathy: I was thinking of some way to get him in trouble, but I didn't know how. And I started reading the paper every morning, and I saw some stories in the paper about that kind of stuff. Then I thought, that's what I want to do, too.

Me: Uh-huh. So you got the idea, then, from the newspaper?

Kathy: Uh-huh.

Me: Okay. As you mentioned before, the notes you wrote to your girlfriend . . .

Kathy: Uh-huh.

Me: Those were all false, then?

Kathy: Uh-huh.

Me: Yeah! Then you mentioned that you didn't think it would go this far?

Kathy: I didn't. I didn't know it would go this far. I knew it would a little ways, and maybe I would get out of the house. But I didn't know all these charges would come up and everything else.

Me: That surprised you?

Kathy: That took me by surprise! I really didn't expect it!

Me: What did you think about that?

Kathy: I was totally blown away when I found out there were charges against him! I was blown away! I didn't know what to do! Didn't know what to think! I decided to go ahead with it still. I didn't know exactly what would happen to him.

Me: Yeah! Yeah! I know you changed your story, you know. You said it did happen, then it didn't happen, then it did happen. You changed it a couple of times before now.

Kathy: Uh-huh.

Me: What you're telling me now is the straight scoop, then?

Kathy: Uh-huh.

Me: This is true information that you did not have sexual intercourse with Michael at all?

Kathy: Uh-huh.

Me: Now, what I want to do is to go and talk with the county attorney. Would you be willing to straighten this out with him now?

Kathy: Yeah!

Me: I know it's embarrassing, all right.

Kathy: It was embarrassing the first time I changed my story.

Me: All right. Someone talked you into continuing on with this story, right?

Kathy: Well, not talked me into it . . . just . . . some people didn't believe when I said nothing happened. So, I thought I was doing a pretty good job of it; maybe I should keep it going. Then he would get in trouble; then my mom would get away from him.

Me: Who do you think you talked to that believed the story and kind of encouraged you to go ahead with more?

Kathy: Well, no one in particular, I mean. I told people it wasn't true, and people said, "I don't believe you. You know we can't force you into saying the real truth, and it did happen."

Me: Who did you talk to that gave you the idea that you should continue?

Kathy: Nobody really! Just all the people I talked to, I guess.

Me: They wanted to hear the worst?

Kathy: Yeah! It sounded like it, anyway; everybody wanted to hear the worst.

Me: Who wanted to hear the worst mostly?

Kathy: Just everybody, I guess. Not one that wanted to hear it mostly. It's just they didn't want to hear it when it didn't happen.

Me: Okay, your story to begin with was phony?

Kathy: Uh-huh.

Me: Is that right?

Kathy: Uh-huh.

Me: Okay, and then when you said it was phony, they didn't believe you?

Kathy: Right!

Me: And so you thought, what the heck, if they believe it was real, then you are going to continue on with it? Is that right?

Kathy: Uh-huh.

Me: It probably made you feel pretty good that they were believing the story?

Kathy: Not pretty good, pretty nervous.

Me: Oh, did it make you feel nervous?

Kathy: Yeah! I was trying to tell the truth, and they didn't believe me. What [was] I going to do?
Me: Uh-huh. And so, what? You thought that you were really going to get back at him because they were believing your story? Is that what I hear you say?
Kathy: Yeah!
Me: Okay, then. Let's go and talk to the attorney.

REVIEW QUESTIONS

1. Do Kathy's responses indicate her desire to rationalize and save face? If so, how might these motivators affect her behavior?

2. Why was Kathy treated so gently?

3. Did acting calm and cool help Kathy in her deception? Give specific examples of times when Kathy was given the opportunity to rationalize and save face.

4. How were the hidden persuaders applied in this inquiry? Give specific examples.

THE CASE OF THE EVASIVE EMBEZZLER
Background

The owner-operator of a small grocery store, which grosses about $500,000 annually, noticed unusual shortages in store income. He contacted me in the hopes of determining the cause of his losses, which he estimated to be excessive. Arrangements were made to interview most of the employees of the store in an effort to determine the cause of those mysterious shortages. The store owner thought employee theft might be involved, and he described in detail the store operations, policies, and personnel. We decided that employee interviews would take place two days after all of the employees were apprised of the investigation.

Several employees cooperated with the investigation, but one tried to avoid the interview. On the morning of her scheduled appointment, she turned in her store keys and announced her resignation. After learning of her refusal to be interviewed, I decided to telephone her and seek her cooperation. Her telephone was busy, so I decided to visit her at home. Based on information I had received and her efforts to avoid me, I decided that my interaction with her would be an interrogation rather than an interview. I was convinced of her involvement in the store's losses. My goal was to gain an admission or confession from her.

I rang the doorbell for her apartment, identified myself to her, and followed her up the stairs to the apartment she shared with her husband and two children. As we went up the stairs, she told me that she was on the telephone and that she would only be a minute. Dogs were barking loudly, and the television was on as I waited near the door inside the apartment. She ended her telephone conversation and asked me to be seated. She closed the door to the apartment and sat across the room from me. The family cat was walking around the living room and came near me; I petted the cat as I began the interaction. Although I identified myself to her at the entrance door, I made certain that she knew my name and purpose so as to avoid confusion during the interaction.

Unknown to her, I was recording the entire interaction on an audiocassette for my own protection and to use for analysis. The use of such a recording device is not legal in all jurisdictions. The text of that interrogation follows. Obviously missing from the transcript is the subtle nonverbal communication that is an essential part of every interaction. However, you can envision the tactics used to gain both compliance and a farewell "thank you" from the subject as I left the apartment. Only she and I were present during the interrogation, which took approximately forty-five minutes to complete. As it turned out, making the recording was quite valuable to both the store owner and myself. The woman later made a claim against the store owner, and I was required to testify in a wrongful termination hearing. Without the recording, it would have been my word against hers. She claimed that I had treated her badly and had misrepresented the results of the interrogation. She lost her claim, primarily because I produced the recording for the mediator to hear.

The Interrogation

Me: Is this a good place to sit?

Subject: Sure.

Me: Okay. Just wanted to explain to you what's going on and so forth, and explain any questions that need to be talked over and that sort of stuff. I'm Chuck Yeschke, and I'm a private investigator, and I'm talking to the employees.

Subject: Uh-huh.

Me: And trying to resolve the shortages that have occurred there.

Subject: Uh-huh.

Me: Apparently, there's several thousand dollars' shortages over the past year or whatever.

Subject: Yeah.

Me: And I don't know if he had an opportunity to explain it to you as well as I hoped that he would.

Subject: He didn't. No. He just said there were shortages in June, and there was again shortages in October.

Me: Okay.

Subject: And that's all he said.

Me: Okay. And then recently, he has been taking a videotape of things going on.

Subject: Uh-huh.

Me: A very, very revealing videotape which you may or may not have known about.

Subject: No, I didn't.

Me: Okay. What I recommended is that he handle it quietly and in-house.

Subject: Uh-huh.

Me: Okay. If at all possible, now my intention is not to embarrass you in any way but certainly to try to resolve this as soon as we can and, you know, work it out.

Subject: Uh-huh, okay.

Me: Okay.

Subject: I don't know if you knew that I quit?

Me: Okay, well you've quit?

Subject: Yes!

Me: Okay, all right. Yes, I got the impression that there was some discussion and he said he was busy with some customers and he was apparently somewhat upset about the discussion. It's not my place to be upset because he's emotionally involved, and so are you and so forth. I'm an outside person. So, what I wanted to do with our discussion today was to talk about merchandise that you've walked off with and not paid for. Let me be sure we understand each other, okay? I've told him that I would prefer to work it out with you and resolve it.

Subject: Uh-huh.

Me: So that there's no doubt as to your cooperation, I'm recommending he not go to the police and make any charge.

Subject: Uh-huh.

Me: Against anyone. That's where I'm coming from, okay? Just to be right up-front with you, okay? There's specific things we have recorded, and I've been involved for a certain period of time, anyway.

Subject: Uh-huh.

Me: So, what I'm looking to do is to resolve, as comfortably as possible for everybody, what involvement they have had with walking off with product, okay?

Subject: Uh-huh.

Me: And just to mention specifically, just so you know where I'm coming from. Just a portion of what I have indicated here. On the first of November as currently as 6:00 P.M. in the evening, a bag of groceries, okay, Old Dutch Potato Chips, and nothing written up but yet the videotape shows the bag leaving in your possession. Okay?

Subject: There was lettuce; there was tomatoes.

Me: Well, okay. Let me be sure! I don't want to press you!

Subject: Yeah, I feel that way though! You got to understand . . .

Me: I do understand that.

Subject: . . . I did pay for it that day!

Me: Okay. Well, it's not written up anywhere! Okay!

Subject: Uh-huh.

Me: Okay, okay. There was a thorough search of all records, and there was nothing paid for! Okay?

Subject: I did though!

Me: Yeah, well, although that's something we need to verify that would have to come out in court, you see. Okay?

Subject: Uh-huh.

Me: All right. Which I think he's willing to do, but I'm saying no! Hold off! I'm trying to say whatever you have not paid for, let's get that resolved and at least indicate your willingness to pay that back and get this straightened out. That's where I'm coming from! All right? I just don't believe it's, you know, thousands and thousands. I don't believe that! All right?

Subject: Uh-huh.

Me: Because I have specific knowledge of who probably has walked off with probably thousands.

Subject: Uh-huh.

Me: Okay, not you, all right?

Subject: Uh-huh.

Me: I'm not putting that on you!

Subject: Uh-huh.

Me: But whatever there is, let's nail that down. Let's get that cleared up so there is no doubt at all where you stand and at least say, hey I'm willing to pay that back and get this straightened out! I'm sorry about that, okay!

Subject: Uh-huh.

Me: That's what I'm trying to say. I like to be in between here and mediate a little bit so he doesn't go too far and you don't get into any bad position! Okay?

Subject: Uh-huh.

Me: All right, and then currently, just to mention these two instances. The second of November, a bag of groceries, Tampax, some sauce, French bread, football stickers, and some tablets. Anyway, now, it's an eight-dollar variety of things definitely not on tape, definitely not rung up, definitely not paid for, but gone and in your possession.

Subject: Uh-huh.

Me: See, that alone is a misdemeanor, all right?

Subject: Uh-huh.

Me: That definitely could be called an embezzlement, it could be a larceny, and it could be a lot of different charges that could be brought by the owner.

Subject: Uh-huh.

Me: Okay, I'm saying back off, give you a chance to straighten things out. Can we do that?

Subject: Yeah.

Me: Okay, what I'm looking to do is to verify with you what you know you've walked off with and you know you haven't paid for, all right? Just right up front, I'd like to do that, all right?

Subject: Okay.

Me: All right. What would be the total amount of any merchandise that you have not paid for? You know, a little bit here, a little bit there, okay? I'm not saying you're carting it off with cases or backing your car up or anything like that, all right? I'm looking at the total picture as best we possibly can, all right? What would that come to if we were to add that up—to look at a total figure as close to the truth as we can come to? We'll put it all in one spot, and we'll say, all right, this is worth . . . whatever that would be? Let's verify to the best of your ability, all right? What would that come to? Would it be two or three thousand dollars' worth? But I don't think so!

Subject: It wouldn't be that high!

Me: Okay, all right, yeah. What I'm talking about is something that we can say is the total maximum, indicate you know this is it, no more than a ceiling limit. What would that come to? If you were to add up the total bits and pieces here and there all in one spot and put a price tag on it? As though, you know, you were to pay for it. What would that come to as far as a value is concerned?

Subject: I don't know. Because . . .

Me: Would it be as much as a thousand dollars?

Subject: No.

Me: Okay, all right. Well now, we have established . . .

Subject: You can't even say a hundred dollars. I can't even say . . .

Me: I don't know. I'm not going to fool around with it. I don't care what it is, all right! I'm saying, let's get that straightened out, whatever it is. If it's under a thousand, you know, then we're dealing with something that can be handled, okay?

Subject: Okay.

Me: If it's a few hundred dollars, well fine. Let's get that straight, all right?

Subject: Okay.

Me: Whatever it is, and I don't care what it is. I just want to be able to say—all right, her intention is honorable; she wants to get it straightened out, all right, all right? Hold off, I'm going to say. That's my first impression to him is, let me talk to her, anyway. Just settle down, okay. He's an excitable guy.

Subject: Yeah!

Me: So, you say it could not be over a thousand. You worked there for how long?

Subject: It will be a year.

Me: Okay, say a year. If it's a dollar a day. Do you follow what I'm trying to say?

Subject: Uh-huh.

Me: A dollar a day, work two hundred days, follow?

Subject: Uh-huh.

Me: A dollar a day, that's four quarters' worth. What can you buy for a dollar?

Subject: Uh-huh.

Me: You know? Ah, one bag of groceries of little bitty stuff equals eight bucks, okay? Okay?

Subject: Uh-huh.

Me: Well, the thing I'm looking at is, you know, if you took eight dollars like that. Small amount! The stuff is so, you know, outrageously priced anywhere!

Subject: Uh-huh.

Me: Let's say it's eight dollars a week.

Subject: Uh-huh.

Me: Okay, fifty-two weeks a year, eight dollars at fifty-two weeks, what's that come to? What does that come to?

Subject (laughing, embarrassed): Don't know.

Me: I don't know. I have a difficult time doing that in my mind, but let's assume. What I'm trying to say is, I'm trying to figure what the total is. That's all I'm doing with you.

Subject: Uh-huh.

Me: If we're looking at fifty-two weeks at eight dollars a week. We've got sixteen, and eight times five is forty—that's $416.00, okay?

Subject: Uh-huh.

Me: Okay, are you following what I'm saying to you? You know, if it's a little bag here and a little bag there. You know what I mean? Occasionally! And the average is that much per week. What would be the average per week? Would it be more than eight, less than eight? About what would it be? What's the most at any one time?

Subject: You mean?

Me: Walked off with, didn't pay for, yeah. What would be the most at any one time? At any one time in the past year if you would look at the total picture and say the biggest bag of whatever you took out was how much? To the best of your knowledge.

Subject: Well, I can't say that because I always paid for my stuff.

Me: Well . . .

Subject: And even those two days, I did pay for it. I paid for it earlier. I knew in my mind what I was going to pick up.

Me: Well, let me be sure you understand something.

Subject: I can't say I took something out without paying for it no matter what size bag it was.

Me: Yeah, well, well . . .

Subject: Because I didn't do that.

Me: Well, that's not the way it is, okay.

Subject: It is, though!

Me: The problem . . .

Subject: As far as that check proving that I paid for everything, except maybe for those two days, but I've got numerous checks here. [Not knowing what to say exactly to convince me that she did not steal, she tripped over her words and made an admission pertaining to not paying.]

Me: I understand, I understand that! What I'm trying to do is establish what the maximum would be that you have not paid for, all right? That's where I'm coming from, okay?

Subject: Uh-huh.

Me: Loud and clear.

Subject: Well, one day he questioned me and he said, uh-huh, he knew exactly what I had. You had a cheeseburger . . .

Me: Let me do this?

Subject: Wait a minute, let me finish.

Me (resigned): Sure.

Subject: Bag of potato chips and a carton of milk, and I said yes. And he said, I didn't see you put any money in [not audible].

Me: Yeah.

Subject: And I said fine, go check, go look at my charge account.

Me: Uh-huh.

Subject: I have a charge account there. He looked, and it was there, and [he] came back and said, yes you do.

Me (sighing): All right, what I'm trying to do now is this, okay? You can decide on whatever you want to do.

Subject: Okay.

Me (speaking slowly): Okay. What I'm trying to do is trying to be in the middle and try to work it out.

Subject (consolingly): I know, I know. Obviously, it's not easy to be stuck in the middle!

Me: Okay, I'd like to avoid as much hassle as possible, okay?

Subject: Uh-huh.

Me: For you and for him and so forth.

Subject: Uh-huh.

Me: He is determined to get this straightened out, okay, and I don't want to see anything go beyond what it has to.

Subject: Yeah.

Me: Okay? I'd just like to appeal to you to get things worked out.

Subject: Yeah.

Me: All right, let me be sure you know where I'm coming from. I'm coming from over thirty years of experience as an investigator. It's obviously clear to me that you walked off and didn't pay for things. Okay? [Spoken in a factual way.] I'm just mentioning these couple, but there are other instances that we have taped on you. [Implied I had a video of her stealing.] Okay? I'm not going to mention that.

Subject: Yeah.

Me: What I'm looking at is why should that come out in court unnecessarily, okay? I'm guaranteeing you that we have enough to go for prosecution. I'm saying to you, please let's straighten out the truth. All right?

Subject: Okay.

Me: All right, I'm not here . . . combat is not what I'm looking for. I'm saying, hey, here it is up front.

Subject: Uh-huh.

Me: You decide! If you say, go jump in the lake, what can I do?

Subject: Yeah.

Me: Then you see you're deciding. I would just as soon that you decide, okay, for you to cause some action that's not very pleasant. Okay, what I'm saying is this now, okay. What I'm looking at is the total picture of all the merchandise that you have not paid for. What would that come to, as far as you're concerned? Oh, I'm looking here. I'm trying to figure out with you, please. If we're looking at, you know, if it's an eight-dollar type of thing once a week, you know, for fifty-two weeks, you know we're looking at $416.00. [I presented myself as being stuck in the middle of this thing—uncomfortable.]

Subject: Uh-huh.

Me: Okay, if that's a fair estimate, fine. Let's establish that, okay?

Subject: All right.

Me: Now, I mean, you know, I want you to know that's where I'm coming from. I'm saying this, I'm just picking that out because it's current, you know, you can remember. Ah, either you used the tampons or you didn't! I mean that's up-to-date!

Subject: Uh-huh.

Me: Okay, so what I'm saying is that's a figure that it looks like we can work with that. All I'm doing is multiplying a year or fifty-two weeks and saying, does that sound fair? Does that sound right? Is that appropriate? I'm asking you that. You tell me! I don't want anybody else to guess! I want you to tell me if it's as accurate, as correct as we can make it.

Subject: Well, I'd have to say no, it's not anywhere near that.

Me: Okay, fine. Let's back off that. What is as accurate, as close to the truth as we can come, then? I mean, maybe it would be, you know, once every two weeks. I don't know this.

Subject: Yeah.

Me: I'm suggesting that we look at the total picture, nail it down, and say, all right. This is as carefully prepared as we can make it. And let's get it straight, okay? All right?

Subject: Yeah.

Me: All right, you say four hundred dollars is too high.

Subject: Oh, yeah, obviously!

Me: All right, what do you think would be as close to the truth as we can make it? Would it be as high as three hundred dollars?

Subject: No.

Me: Okay, all right. What I'm saying now is merchandise that you walked off with, didn't pay for. And that's what we're talking about, all right?

Subject: Uh-huh.

Me: All right, it's in a reasonable area we can talk about; it's not world-shaking. It's not inexpensive, certainly; but it's within reason we can work out! Okay? Good! Okay? Could two hundred dollars cover it? Do you think that two hundred dollars would be as close as we could come to the truth? Maximum? No doubt about it? No more than two hundred dollars. About two hundred dollars, but not any more? Is that fair?

Subject: No, I guess that isn't either!

Me: Okay. Well, tell me then. What would be as fair and accurate as we can make it? Under two hundred dollars? What is as fair as you can recall on that amount that you have not paid for and walked off with and so forth. What would that be?

Subject: I don't know. Because I still say I paid for my stuff! I might not have paid when I actually took the bottle of pop or when I took the candy.

Me: I'm talking about walking out with it, okay? That means not paying for it at all, okay? That's what I'm saying to you. Where the company would not be getting any money for the product. But the product is gone because you took it, all right?

Subject: Okay.

Me: All right, okay.

Subject: But I still have to say in those instances, the ones when you came up with the potato chips stuff, I did pay for it! I did pay for it! I know I put the money in there. I took it out of money that I always have, money in my purse. My wallet got stolen from me so I started carrying money with me. But I do have checks to verify that . . .

Me: Okay, okay. What I'm looking at is what you're willing to straighten out and verify, okay?

Subject: Uh-huh.

Me: Okay, the pure simple truth of the matter is that I don't really need to be here!

Subject: Uh-huh, but I also have to defend myself.

Me: I know that! Oh, my dear, I know that. I know that! That's no problem. You may defend yourself. I'd rather you do it here than in court, all right?

Subject: I guess the thing is that I don't believe he's doing it. I've made bank deposits for him over the year.

Me: I know.

Subject: If I was going to take something . . .

Me: I know.

Subject (beginning to cry): I would have taken it there.

Me: Okay, I realize that. What I'm trying to say to you is, let us clarify what the truth . . .

Subject (crying but not defeated): Let him keep my check. He owes me for a week; let him keep it. That should take care of anything I owe him.

Me: What I'm concerned about is this. I'm not here to make you upset, please.

Subject: I have been since he told me this.

Me (consolingly): I know, okay. The thing I'm concerned about is trying to work it out. To work it out as comfortably as you can, but I know it's not comfortable. I know that!

Subject: But if that's going to make him feel like I have sufficiently paid for it, let him keep the check. Because that's all I can do. I can't pay for something I know I paid for.

Me: Uh-huh. Have you talked to your husband yet? [Diversion question.]

Subject: I mean to. I told him I quit, but I haven't told him about this.

Me: Okay. Okay, well, all I can do is ask if you would clarify what you know you have not paid for, what you have taken and so forth, to the best of your knowledge. And you say it is under two hundred dollars. Do you think two hundred dollars would cover it or one hundred dollars, or what would be the maximum total of any that you know that you still owe for what you've taken?

Subject: Okay, what I still owe for is in my charge at work, which is maybe fifteen dollars. Because that's the only thing I've ever walked out that door with . . . I didn't hide them from him or anything.

Me: I understand that, I understand that, but a . . .

Subject: And I did pay for it!

Me: Yeah, uh-huh. Well, after a full search, that's not the case! Okay, what I hear you say then is . . . I don't even know how much that check is worth that you have there. What is that worth?

Subject: I don't know. I get four dollars per hour. A hundred and fifty dollars.

Me: Okay.

Subject: So, if he wants to just keep it, he can!

Me: That would even things out, do you think?

Subject: Yeah, I don't know. I mean, it will probably make things fine with him. I don't know, but it's not going to make things right with me.

Me: I understand. As far as you're concerned, okay, we're not dealing with thousands of dollars. We're dealing with about that much, and you think that would cover it, and then it would be an even type thing. That's what I hear you say!

Subject: Well, yeah, as far as he's concerned, I know what I've done. I haven't! I mean. He told me this wasn't going to be humiliating. Of course it is!

Me: The whole thing is uncomfortable, no doubt. It's uncomfortable. No doubt about it. It's an obviously uncomfortable situation for anybody to be in. And I'm trying to say, hey, let's make it as comfortable as we can. And that's why I'm suggesting to him and you ways to work it out.

Subject: Yeah.

Me: Okay, that's what I'm saying to you.

Subject: [Not audible] let him keep the check [not audible].

Me: I'm making a note out to him so that he knows what you and I talked about, okay? And you read it over in just a minute so that it's clear to you too.

Let me read this to you here. I'm addressing it to him. "Dear Mr._____. I have quit _____ grocery today. I have given up my keys. I want _____ to keep my paycheck if he thinks it will cover the merchandise I have taken from the store without paying for it. I believe that the check in holding is about $150. I believe we are even then. I will make no claim for that last paycheck. I won't bother with it. Mr. Yeschke has treated me fairly today. No one has promised me anything or threatened me in any way to make this statement." Okay, so is that straightforward?

Subject: Yeah, but it's still implying that I'm saying that I did it. And I'm saying that I didn't do it. So, all I'm saying is, if that's what is going to make him happy, keeping it, then fine.

Me: I understand.

Subject: But I'm not going to admit that I did something!

Me: I understand.

Subject: I still say I didn't.

Me: Okay. I'll put that in there, okay? "I refuse to admit that I stole from _____ grocery; but I am willing to allow _____ grocery to keep my last paycheck."

I really haven't talked with him too much, but he did show concern when I did speak with him. Okay, let's see (reading over statement to self). Okay, let me read this: "I refuse to admit that I stole from _____ grocery, but I'm willing to allow Mr. _____ of _____ grocery to keep my last paycheck. I believe this is the only fair thing to do. I have clear thoughts regarding this matter." In other words, you're thinking on it and you're as clear as you can be on this, okay? Why don't you read this over if you will? (Statement and pen given to subject.) I scratched one word down there at the very end if you would put your initials by that, at least. I'll tell you what. Would you write, "The above is the truth," just underneath there, and put your name underneath that? Indicating that you've read it.

Thank you! (She returned signed statement.) The main thing is that you know you're indicating your willingness to get it straightened out, and I would think that it would be enough! Okay.

Subject: I don't think it will be!

Me: You don't think so? You think he's the kind of guy that's going to be pushy or something? Well, let's hope this will work out as smoothly as possible. That's my recommendation, anyway. This is hopefully running its course as it is here.

Subject: What's going to happen next?

Me: Well, I can't say that because I don't know. It's not up to me. I have no control over that. It's not up to me. I wish I could give you some easy answer, but I don't have any easy answers. Do you have a child? [Diversion question.]

Subject (crying): I have two.

Me: Two children. Not very good times for this problem for you!

Subject (crying): I don't believe he did this. I don't believe it. I do not believe it. I think what bothers me the most is that I worked with him, I've worked with his wife; I trained in his wife. Me and his wife became friends, and for him to do this—I don't believe it.

Me: Yeah.

Subject (crying): I know he isn't going to be satisfied with this. I know that every time I go for a job, he's going to hurt me. I know it. I've taken care of other people's kids; I've been a Sunday school teacher; I've been a Bible school teacher; I'm a Brownie leader now for twelve girls. And then for him to come along and do this to me.

Me: I know it's not easy, not easy. Well, to verify just the fact that it would be some minor amounts as you've indicated here . . .

Subject: [Not audible]

Me: Okay, as far as I'm concerned, you know, all I can do is what we've done now, and leave it go at that. It would be up to Mr. _____ to talk with you or you to him or whatever. It's important, I think, for you to talk to your husband and get things worked out. Anyway, that's a possibility for some time in the future. If you have any questions, please give me a call. And as I say, I'm kind of in the middle and trying to work things as smoothly as possible so that . . .

Subject: I didn't mean to cry. It's just that there's a lot of tension on me.

Me: I know there's a lot of tension on you. That's okay. It's a normal thing for you to cry; you must feel pretty much alone . . .

Subject (crying): [Not audible]

Me: You probably feel disappointed too?

Subject: That's the biggest thing. I never called in sick or took time off because I knew he was stuck. I worked when they were on vacation. [Some comments not audible]

Me: Yeah. That's the real painful part of it is when you give up part of yourself and something like this occurs.

Subject: He gave me lousy jobs, and I did them . . . [Not audible]

Me: Well, I appreciate your time, and I'm sorry we have you feeling upset; but as I say, I'm trying to be somewhat in the middle and try to work it out the best way we can. I know it's not easy for you, I realize that. But if there's any questions you have or if there's . . .

Subject: I have a bank key.

Me: Bank key? Do you have it now? I can carry it to him.

Subject: [Not audible, no denial]

Me: Well, if you prefer, if you want to drop if off there.

Subject: I'll just give it to you!

Me: It is a bank key, is it?

Subject: [Not audible]

Me: Okay, I'll talk with him and explain, you are trying to be cooperative, and there's a certain hesitance, a feeling of needing to be protective and so forth, and that's understood. That's understood. Anyway, if there's anything that I can comment on, feel free to give me a call.

Subject: Are you going to call and let me know [not audible]

Me: Let me talk with him and see what the circumstances are, and my recommendation to him will be that it stops here, okay? Even though you were reluctant to admit stealing, I can see where you're coming from, and that's understood. But you have in so many words told me that you have, and you know, that's neither here nor there. I mean, you don't have to really say it specifically. I'm convinced that you have and that you have already explained, and $150 covers it, and so forth, and, you know, that's what I hear you saying. Okay?

Subject: [Not audible]

Me: I know, I know that you didn't specifically say that, I know that. But what I'm looking to do is to explain to him that you're clearing this up reasonably, and I'm getting the clear impression that you're sorry for, you know, walking off with product, and you're disappointed that it had to come to this stage. And that's about all. Okay?

Subject: [Not audible]

Me: I'll talk to him, then, and try to get things worked out the best way possible. Anything else you want to ask me before I leave?

Subject: No.

Me: I haven't abused you in any way, I hope, okay?

Subject: No.

Me: Okay, I just want to be sure I treated you fairly in discussing it and trying to straighten things out. Is that what I hear you say?

Subject: Yeah.

Me: Okay, because I don't want to upset you any more than you already are. Take care now!
Subject: Okay.
Me: Bye-bye.
Subject: Bye. Thank you!
Me: Uh-huh.

REVIEW QUESTIONS

1. How did the investigator establish rapport in this inquiry?

2. Did the subject of the interrogation ever specifically deny stealing from the store? If not, why not?

3. Did the investigator lie to the subject? If so, when and how?

4. What did it mean when the subject began to cry?

5. Was the subject's statement voluntary?

6. How did the subject try to save face, and when?

7. Why did the investigator indicate that he was convinced she had stolen from her employer?

8. How were the hidden persuaders applied in this inquiry? Give specific examples.

Conclusion

There is, it seems, much confusion over the law regarding the dif ferences between private and public interviewing. It is my hope that this book may, in some small way, help progressive policy-makers see more clearly what investigative interviewing consists of and how it affects both private and public investigations so that they can advance acceptable guidelines for all investigators. Clearly defined standards for interviewing and interrogating will strengthen the role of both private and public investigators. We have waited far too long for such guidelines.

It is my hope and prayer that this book will make it obvious and indisputable that the way you treat people influences their responses. Finally, I suggest that you learn how to whistle for the truth while using finesse.

Soli Deo Gloria.

Bibliography

Abrams, Stanley. 1977. *A Polygraph Handbook for Attorneys*. Lexington, Mass.: Lexington Books.

Adorno, T. W., Else Frenkel-Brunswik, Daniel F. Levinson, and R. Nevitt. 1950. *The Authoritarian Personality*. New York: Sanford, Harper and Brothers.

American Polygraph Association. 1990. Code of Ethics and Standards and Principles of Practice.

American Psychiatric Association. 1980. *Diagnostic and Statistical Manual of Mental Disorders*. 3d ed. Washington, D.C.: APA.

Aubry, Arthur S., Jr., and Rudolph R. Caputo. 1980. *Criminal Interrogation*. Springfield, Ill.: Charles C Thomas.

Banaka, William H. 1971. *Training in Depth Interviewing*. New York: Harper and Row.

Beckwith v. United States, 425 U.S. 341, 96 S. Ct. 1612 (1976).

Benjamin, Alfred. 1974. *The Helping Interview*. Boston: Houghton-Mifflin.

Bennis, W. G., D. E. Berlew, E. H. Schein, and F. I. Steel, eds. 1973. *Interpersonal Dynamics: Essays and Readings on Human Interaction.* 3d ed. Homewood, Ill.: Dorsey Press.

Berg, Irwin A., and Bernard M. Bass, eds. 1961. *Conformity and Deviation.* New York: Harper and Brothers.

Berne, Eric. 1974. *Games People Play.* New York: Grove.

Berne, Eric. 1977. *Intuition and Ego States.* San Francisco, TA Press.

Binder, D. A., and S. C. Price. 1977. *Legal Interviewing and Counseling.* St. Paul, Minn.: West.

Birdwhistell, R. L. 1970. *Kinesics and Content: Essays on Body Communication.* Philadelphia: University of Pennsylvania Press.

Boorstin, Daniel. 1972. *The Image.* New York: Atheneum.

Bowers, David A. 1976. *Systems of Organization.* Ann Arbor: University of Michigan Press.

Brady, John. 1977. *The Craft of Interviewing.* New York: Vantage.

Brewer v. Williams, 430 U.S. 387, 97 S. Ct. 1232 (1977).

Bridgeman, Percy W., and Gerald Holton. 1982. "Scientific Methods." *McGraw-Hill Encyclopedia of Science and Technology.* 5th ed. New York: McGraw-Hill.

Bynum, W. F., E. J. Browne, and Roy Porter. 1982. *Dictionary of the History of Science.* Princeton, N.J.: Princeton University Press.

California v. Prysock, 453 U.S. 355, 101 S. Ct. 2806 (1981).

Cameron, Norman, and Ann Margaret Cameron. 1951. *Behavior Pathology.* Boston: Riverside Press.

Cavanagh, Michael E. 1979. *How to Handle Your Anger.* 4th ed. Washington, D.C.: U.S. Dept. of Labor, Employment and Training Administration.

City of Grand Rapids v. Impens, 32 Cr. L. 2308 (Mich. Sup. Ct. 1982).

Cleckley, Hervey M. 1976. *The Mask of Sanity: An Attempt to Clarify Some Issues about the So-Called Sociopathic Personality.* 5th ed. St. Louis, Mo.: Mosby.

Cocke, E. W. 1953. Constitutional psychopathic personality in relation to present-day crime and delinquency. *The Peace Officer* 10(1):130.

Coleman, James C. 1976. *Abnormal Psychology and Modern Life.* 5th ed. Glenview, Ill.: Scott, Foresman.

Communication: The Nonverbal Agenda. 1975. New York: McGraw-Hill Films.

Davis, Flora. 1975. *Inside Intuition.* New York: New American Library, Times Mirror.

Dello, E. L. 1970. *Methods of Science.* New York: Universe.

Dewey, John. 1957. *Human Nature and Conduct.* New York: Modern Library.

Dexter, Lewis Anthony. 1970. *Elite and Specialized Interviewing.* Evanston, Ill.: Northwestern University Press.

Dougherty, George S. 1924. *The Criminal as a Human Being.* New York: Appleton.

Downs, Cal W., G. Paul Smeyak, and Ernest Martin. 1980. *Professional Interviewing.* New York: Harper and Row.

Drake, John D. 1972. *Interviewing for Managers: Sizing up People.* New York: American Management Association.

Dunaway v. New York, 442 U.S. 200, 99 S. Ct. 2248 (1979).

Eden, D., and J. Kinnar. 1991. Modeling Galatea: Boosting self-efficacy to increase volunteering. *Journal of Applied Psychology* 76(6): 770–80.

The Effective Uses of Power and Authority. 1980. New York: McGraw-Hill Films.

Egler, Frank E. 1970. *The Way of Science.* New York: Hafner.

Empathy in Police Work. 1972. Produced by L. Craig Jr. Madison, Conn. Film.

The Empowerment Series. 1992. Carlsbad, Calif.: CRM Films.

Ethical Code of the Medical Profession, 2001.

Federal Bureau of Investigation. 2001. *Crime in the United States.* Washington, D.C.: U.S. Government Printing Office.

Fischer, Frank E. 1955. A new look at management communications. *Personnel* 31:487–495.

Frazier v. Cupp, 394 U.S. 731, 89 S. Ct. 1420 (1969).

Freeman, G. L., E. T. Katzoff, G. E. Manson, and J. H. Pathman. 1942. The stress interview. *Journal of Abnormal and Social Psychology* 37: 427–447.

Freeman, H., and H. Weihofen. 1972. *Clinical Law Training: Interviewing and Counseling.* St. Paul, Minn.: West.

Garrett, Annette. 1972. *Interviewing: Its Principles and Methods.* New York: Family Service Association of America.

Gist, M. E. 1987. Self-efficacy: Implications for organizational behavior and human resource management. *Academy of Management Review* 12(3): 472–485.

Gorden, Raymond L. 1969. *Interviewing: Strategy, Techniques, and Tactics.* Homewood, Ill.: Dorsey Press.

Gunn, Battiscombe. 1918. *The Instruction of PTAH-HOTEP and the Instruction of KE'GEMNI: The Oldest Books in the World.* West London: John Murray.

Hall, E. T. 1966. *The Hidden Dimension.* New York: Doubleday.

Harre, Ron, and Roger Lamb, eds. 1983. *The Encyclopedic Dictionary of Psychology.* Cambridge, Mass.: MIT Press.

Harris, Thomas A. 1973. *I'm Okay—You're Okay: A Practical Guide to Transactional Analysis.* Distributed by Success Motivation Institute, Inc., New York, by special arrangement with R. M. Karen and Harper and Row. Videotape.

Harryman v. Estelle, 616 F.2d 870 (5th Cir. 1980).

Hess, Kären M., and Henry M. Wrobleski. 1988. *For the Record: Report Writing in Law Enforcement.* Eureka, Calif.: Innovative Systems.

Inbau, Fred, John Reid, and Joseph Buckley. 1986. *Criminal Interrogation and Confessions.* 3d ed. Baltimore: Williams and Wilkins.

I Understand, You Understand. 1975. Des Moines: Creative Media. Film.

Kahn, Robert L., and Charles F. Cannell. 1957. *The Dynamics of Interviewing: Theory, Technique, and Cases.* New York: Wiley.

Karp, H. B., and Bob Abramms. 1992. Doing the right thing. *Training and Development* (August): 37–41.

Keefe, William F. 1971. *Listen Management.* New York: McGraw-Hill.

Kellihan, S. J. 1982. Searching for the meaning of the truth and the ethics of its use. Speech presented at the annual seminar of the American Polygraph Association.

Kleinmuntz, Benjamin. 1974. *Essentials of Abnormal Psychology.* New York: Harper and Row.

Knapp, Mark. 1972. *Nonverbal Communication.* New York: Holt, Rinehart and Winston.

Kubler-Ross, Elizabeth. 1969. *On Death and Dying.* New York: Macmillan.

Levere, Trevor H. 1995. "Science." *Collier's Encyclopedia.*

Lopez, Felix. 1975. *Personnel Interviewing.* New York: McGraw-Hill.

Mallory, James D., Jr. 1977. *The Kink and I.* Wheaton, Ill.: Victor.

Maltz, Maxwell. 1960. *Psycho-cybernetics.* Englewood Cliffs, N.J.: Prentice-Hall.

Man and His Values: An Inquiry into Good and Evil. 1972. Center for Humanities. Videotape.

Maslow, Abraham H. 1954. *Motivation and Personality.* New York: Harper.

McClelland, David. 1976. *Motivational Management.* Boston: Forum Corporation.

McCormick, Charles T. 1954. *Evidence.* Hornbook Series. St. Paul, Minn.: West.

McGregor, Douglas Murray. 1960. *The Human Side of Enterprise.* New York: McGraw-Hill.

Menninger, William C. 1953. *What Makes an Effective Man.* Personnel Series, no. 152. New York: American Management Association.

Minnick, Wayne C. 1985. *The Art of Persuasion.* Boston: Houghton Mifflin.

Miranda v. Arizona, 384 U.S. 436, 86 S. Ct. 1602 (1966).

Nierenberg, Gerard I. 1968. *The Art of Negotiating.* New York: Cornerstone.

Nirenberg, Jesse S. 1963. *Getting through to People.* Englewood Cliffs, N.J.: Prentice-Hall.

Nonverbal Communication. 1976. New York: Harper and Row. Film.

Officer Stress Awareness. 1976. New York: Harper and Row. Film.

Oregon v. Mathiason, 429 U.S. 492, 97 S. Ct. 711 (1977).

Orozco v. Texas, 394 U.S. 324, 89 S. Ct. 1095 (1969).

OSS Assessment Staff. 1948. *Assessment of Men: Selection of Personnel for the Office of Strategic Services.* New York: Rinehart.

Petry, Edward. 1990. Have we lost our moral compass? *The Corporate Ethics and the Environment.* Waltham, Mass.: Bentley College Press.

Phillips, D. L., and K. Clancy. 1972. Modeling effects in survey research. *Public Opinion Quarterly* 36(2): 246–253.

Productivity and the Self-Fulfilling Prophecy: The Pygmalion Effect. 1975. New York: McGraw-Hill Films.

Quinn, L., and N. Zunin. 1972. *Contact: The First Four Minutes.* Los Angeles: Nash.

Reusch, Jurgen, and Weldon Kees. 1954. *Nonverbal Communication.* Berkeley: University of California Press.

Rhode Island v. Innes, 446 U.S. 291, 100 S. Ct. 1682 (1980).

Rogers, Carl R. 1942. *Counseling and Psychotherapy.* Boston: Houghton Mifflin.

Ross, Alec, and David Plant. 1979. *Writing Police Reports: A Practical Guide.* Schiller Park, Ill.: Motorola Teleprograms.

Royal, Robert F., and Steven R. Schutt. 1976. *The Gentle Art of Interviewing and Interrogation.* Englewood Cliffs, N.J.: Prentice Hall.

Sapir, Edward. 1949. *Selected Writings of Edward Sapir.* Edited by D. G. Mandelbaum. Berkeley and Los Angeles: University of California Press.

Scheflen, A. E. 1964. Significance of posture in communications systems. *Psychiatry* 27(4): 316–331.

Schultz, William C. 1966. *The Interpersonal Underworld.* Palo Alto, Calif.: Science and Behavior Books.

"The Sciences." N.d. Vertical file, Literature Department, Minneapolis Public Library, Minneapolis, Minnesota.

Selling to Tough Customers. 1981. Del Mar, Calif.: McGraw-Hill Films.

Selye, Hans. 1975. *Stress without Distress.* New York: American Library.

Shaw, George Bernard. 1994. *Pygmalion.* 1912. Reprint, Mineola, N.Y.: Dover.

Sherwood, Hugh. 1972. *The Journalistic Interview.* New York: Harper and Row.

Simons, Hebert W. 1976. *Persuasion.* Reading, Mass.: Addison-Wesley.

Sipe, H. Craig. 1985. "Science." *World Book Encyclopedia.*

Social Security Administration. 1964. *Interviewing and Counseling.* Washington, D.C.: U.S. Dept. of Health, Education and Welfare, Social Security Administration.

Stewart, Charles J., and William B. Cash. 1974. *Interviewing: Principles and Practices.* Dubuque, Iowa: William C. Brown.

———. 1978. *Interviewing.* Dubuque, Iowa: William C. Brown.

Thompson, George N. 1953. *The Psychopathic Delinquent and Criminal.* Springfield, Ill.: Charles C Thomas.

Toffler, Alvin. 1970. *Future Shock.* New York: Random House.

Wicks, Robert J., and Ernest H. Josephs Jr. 1972. *Techniques in Interviewing for Law Enforcement and Corrections Personnel.* Springfield, Ill.: Charles C Thomas.

Woody, Robert H., and Jane D. Woody, eds., 1972. *Clinical Assessment in Counseling and Psychotherapy.* New York: Appleton, Century, Crofts, Meredith.

Yeschke, Charles L. 1962. The advantages and limitations of police applicant testing with the polygraph. Paper presented at the ninth annual meeting of the American Academy of Polygraph Examiners, Chicago.

———. 1963. Ethical considerations for polygraph examiners. Paper presented at the tenth annual meeting of the American Academy of Polygraph Examiners, Chicago.

———. 1965. Ethics and the polygraph examiner. *Journal of Criminal Law, Criminology and Police Science* 56(1):109–112.

———. 1981a. A bargain for life: Basics of hostage negotiations. *Ohio Police* (December):23–39.

———. 1981b. Effective interviewing: A skill no officer can afford to be without. *Minnesota Sheriff* 19(4):29–81.

———. 1981c. Why you shouldn't forget about that $1200 embezzlement. *Commercial West* (January 24):12–13.

———. 1982a. Coping with the artful dodgers: A guide for the polygraph investigator. *Minnesota Police Chief* 2(3):49–55.

———. 1982b. Nice guys make better interviewers. *Law and Order* 30(8): 67–69.

———. 1982c. The polygraph dodger. *Minnesota Sheriff* 20(3):23–27.

———. 1982d. What to do when bank managers suspect employees of embezzlement. *Commercial West* (October 9):12–33.

———. 1982e. Written security policies can stem theft by bank employees. *Commercial West* (June 26):20–33.

———. 1983. Positive use of power in police interviewing/interrogating. *Law and Order* 31(9):67–70.

————. 1984. The cost of interviewing. *Tell It A.S.I.S.* (newsletter of the Central Minnesota Chapter of the American Society for Industrial Security) 2(1):1–4.

————. 1985a. Innocence, bravery, and reality: A tribute to John Scanlon. *Minnesota Police Chief* 5(3):47–49.

————. 1985b. Interviewing door-to-door: In search of the elusive. *Illinois Police Officer* 16(3):149–155.

————. 1985c. Polygraphy: A unique profession. *Minnesota Freelancer* 1(2):26–28.

————. 1988. Banking on police and polygraphy. *Commercial West* 173(36):14–15.

————. 1989a. Fraud/embezzlement: What to do? Paper presented at a conference of the Independent Bankers of Minnesota, Bloomington.

————. 1989b. Local police and polygraphy. *Minnesota Police Chief* 9(1): 123–133.

————. 1993. *Interviewing: A Forensic Guide to Interrogation.* 2d ed. Springfield, Ill.: Charles C Thomas.

Zuckerman, Harriet. 1977. *Scientific Elite.* London: The Free Press, Collier Macmillan.

Index

Page references followed by "f" denote figures.